Reflections on the Futures of Marketing

➤ ➤ ➤ ➤ ➤ ➤ ➤

Reflections on the Futures of Marketing

➤ ➤ ➤ ➤ ➤ ➤ ➤

Practice and Education

edited by Donald R. Lehmann and Katherine E. Jocz

Marketing Science Institute
Cambridge, MA

Contents

Editors' Note

The essays in this volume were conceived as a concerted attempt to reflect on changes occurring in the field of marketing. The principal contributors are all former executive directors of the Marketing Science Institute (MSI)—senior marketing professors who understand the interface between theory-driven research, teaching, and practice.

At the outset, the questions posed were: How did marketing as discipline and practice get to where it is now? What is its current status? Where is it likely to go from here? The resultant thinking has significant implications for practice, academic research, and education and professional development in marketing.

We chose the title as the plural futures of marketing, at the suggestion of Professor Alice Tybout, to reflect both uncertainty and multiple scenarios that may play out in different aspects of marketing. Early on we also decided that "future" would not be "futuristic." The time horizon here is approximately 5 to 10 years out and hence the future is largely extrapolated from present forces and trends. While there are uncertainties (e.g., political turmoil, epidemics) that could significantly change the role of marketing, we did not see ourselves as particularly able to forecast developments that do not exist in any form today. We also do not claim that this book is a comprehensive treatment of marketing. Rather the volume is a series of thoughtful and thought-stimulating reflections on different facets of marketing as it enters the 21st century.

There are many who deserve thanks. The past executive directors, the academic trustees, and the executive and research policy committees of MSI all gave valuable advice at the beginning of the project. In

November 1995, versions of the papers were presented to the MSI
Trustees, who provided many insightful comments. Robert Blattberg
and Richard Staelin contributed their ideas, and Stephan Haeckel,
David Montgomery, and Paul Root supported the effort throughout.
We also gratefully acknowledge Susan Keane and Michele Kennedy,
respectively, for their skillful assistance in editing and designing this
volume.

Donald R. Lehmann
Columbia University

Katherine E. Jocz
Marketing Science Institute

Preface

Stephan H. Haeckel

It is hard to come away from this book without a strong conviction that marketing's future is not as *a* function of business, but as *the* function of business. The "marketing concept," we learn from Stephen Greyser, has many fathers on both the practicing and academic sides of the family tree. It has several formulations, and is at least four decades old. In Greyser's terms, its essence is making customers, rather than another constituency, the alpha and omega of business focus. That is, what a firm does should be grounded on the best possible understanding of customer wants and needs—latent, tacit, and articulated. Similarly, the assessment of how well a firm performs should be made by the customer, in customer terms. A major premise is that the interests of all other stakeholders—which include employees, society, and owners—are best served in the long term by treating them as the consequence, rather than the focus, of business activity.

Having reminded us of the marketing concept's pedigree and persistence, the authors proceed to provide us with strategic insights of such scope that affixing a marketing label to them seems both arbitrary and inadequate. Marketing straddles strategy, tactics, and culture, and should be thought of as a process, says Frederick Webster. He argues persuasively that strategies dominated by competitor focus and internal/financially oriented thinking have led to a crippling disconnect between the culture and tactics of many firms.

George Day adds "boundaries," "growth," and "knowledge" to Webster's "process" as the critical elements for firms to manage in the future—a far cry from the 4Ps and marketing mix that were once thought to circumscribe marketing's decision-making domain. Day asks, "Where will deep market knowledge . . . be located, and how will it be provided to the rest of the organization?" In his thoughtful discussion of this question, Day takes us through several alternatives, each constituting a plausible scenario for the future of marketing.

John Farley offers a rich harvest of insights into the growth segments of the global marketplace. If you aren't thinking about the developing economies of Latin America, Southeast Asia, and China—where the average age is one half, and the economic growth rate about twice, that of developed market economies—you may want to rethink what markets to think about. And, speaking of rethinking, Bob Buzzell and Rajendra Sisodia provide much food for thinking about what we need to teach and learn in the business schools of the future.

After these minds finish with the futures of marketing, it's difficult to imagine many interesting issues that might remain for a book on the futures of business. The fact that these authors stay within the "confines" of the marketing concept says a great deal about its robustness and relevance across the spectrum of business strategy. It also raises questions about the robustness and relevance of marketing as a profession. Has marketing, as Fred Webster asked in 1989, become too important to be left to the marketers? Will the future of the marketing department, wonders Don Lehmann, be reduced to responsibility for managing cents-off promotions?

Though the latter questions are duly and imaginatively addressed in this book, they turn out to be of less strategic interest than the authors' revelations about why the venerable marketing concept is so pertinent today, and promising for tomorrow.

➤

Given that several decades have passed since the marketing concept's original formulations, what's new—or at least different—this time around? Is there, in fact, any reason to believe that this generation's executives will be better than their predecessors at ensuring that customer-centric behavior actually occurs? Some would argue that the history of the marketing concept, with a few notable exceptions, is more prose than practice—rhetorical marketing lipstick painted on a product-centered, profit-maximizing economic pig. How many executives, they ask, would formulate the essential function of their business as "meeting customer wants and needs, with profit as a constraint" (as opposed to "making a profit by producing products and services that come closer than competitors to meeting customer needs")? And how many of those who formulate it the first way would be able to demonstrate consistent measurements and reward systems?

At issue is: Who is the firm's primary constituency? Whose interest will be prioritized most frequently when there is a conflict? Many companies don't care to become either explicit or consistent about this, preferring the flexibility that comes with ambiguity. Johnson and Johnson is a celebrated exception. Their decades-old "credo," which you can find posted in almost any J&J office, establishes the pecking order very unambiguously: customers first, then employees, then communities, and finally shareholders. The clarity of the credo—and the consistency of the J&J reward system—is credited with the astounding speed with which all bottles of Tylenol were removed from retail shelves when it became known that a few had been tampered with. CEO James Burke did not have to send out an executive order—he did not, really, even have to make a decision. It had been made in 1943 when Robert Johnson produced the credo. And every J&J employee from chairman to route salesman, apparently, understood it and acted accordingly.

What, to return to the question of what's different now, might cause Robert Johnson's priorities to become the norm, rather than the exception? The leading candidate is *a change in the nature of change:*

from continuous (but incremental) to discontinuous. In sufficiently stable environments, there is really not much difference between product- and customer-centric businesses. Both the shareholder and the customer benefit directly and in the short term from investments that enhance the efficiency and productivity with which accurately forecasted demand in well-segmented markets is met by defined products and services. But when discontinuous change makes customer requests unpredictable, strategic leverage shifts from efficiency to flexibility and responsiveness—and to investments that enable a firm to sense unanticipated change earlier and coordinate an unprecedented response to it faster.

If this type of "sense and respond" imperative were actually replacing "predict, make, and sell," we could expect to hear managers talking about customer intimacy, customer profitability, customer lifetime value, and customer relationship management. We would see them investing in flexible manufacturing systems and mass customization capabilities. We would be reading about $6 billion companies like Eli Lilly paying $4 billion to McKesson for a $100 million subsidiary in order to acquire a database of consumer transactions—dramatic testimony to a growing understanding that "ownership" of future customers will depend on who senses their wants and needs earliest and most completely. This book provides ample and credible evidence that the marketing concept is in fact becoming the business concept, and suggests that executives give serious thought to structuring their firms around different types of customers rather than brands or geographies. This would put them on the same page as Jim Burke, who said in 1981 that J&J's basic organizational philosophy "is to try to organize each business around a given market need and a given set of customers. It's easier said than done but that's really it."

➤

Given the nature of discontinuous, nonlinear change, much of the relevant thinking about the future of business is rooted in nonmarketing—even nonbusiness—disciplines. Marketing, which has always made liberal use of the tools of other disciplines, must now consider borrowing more of their metaphors and models. The idea of transforming a business from an efficient mechanism for making offers into an adaptive organism for generating responses amounts to a different way of thinking about the essential function of business.

It wasn't until well into this century that physicists faced up squarely to the fact that their idealized models were inadequate to explain most of what really goes on in the world. This is not to gainsay the value of Newtonian mechanics, which provided good enough approximations for an enormous amount of technological progress, as well as for the mechanistic, command-and-control business concepts of the industrial age. The information age, however, came to pass because of quantum theory, that collection of incredibly counterintuitive abstractions underlying the physics and chemistry of the now-ubiquitous computer chip.

As marketing and business come to grips with the strategic and structural issues of managing in an information economy, it seems a foregone conclusion that we, like physicists before us, will have to import radically new concepts upon which to build a new model. Why shouldn't we expect the form and function of an information age organization to be at least as different from its industrial age counterpart as the factory was from the farm?

Some of the most provocative and compelling ideas are coming from unlikely sources: chaos and complexity theory, social anthropology, linguistics, cognitive and computer science, and epistemology. Is it likely that existing marketing organizations—either in business or academe—will become the spawning ground and synthesizing agency for the interdisciplinary research needed to apply these concepts to business? If not, what kind of external agency will be required?

In universities the marketing department tends, I am told, to be a house divided into "quantitative" and "behavioral" camps. More generally, business school courses—and research—that integrate organizational behavior, strategy, marketing, and finance are the exception. Many marketing thinkers are convinced that business strategy and organizational behavior are now separate disciplines because marketing, years ago, failed to include them in an expanded understanding of the issues embraced by marketing. And Webster, in his chapter, expresses the collective embarrassment of the marketing function that it was not marketing, but operations, that initiated and drove the quality movement. Given the width and depth of the internal intellectual chasms that afflict business schools, how can we reasonably expect them to catalyze an effort to span the abysses separating business, science, engineering, and liberal arts schools?

Nor, on the business side, is there much evidence to date that the marketing concept will be entrusted to the marketing function. To the contrary, in many firms great chunks of marketing's putative domain have been torn off and transplanted into separate operations, e.g., brand management, communications, advertising, channel management, strategic planning, market intelligence, and so on. And many of the newer issues like organizational learning, services quality, intellectual capital management, and globalization spend little or no time under the aegis of the marketing department.

Perhaps the function is withering away in some kind of Marxian consequence of its total triumph—another data point supporting Walter Lippmann's dictum that "nothing recedes like success." Or perhaps, as some charge, marketing has relinquished leadership because it systematically prioritizes specialization over generalization, rewarding academics and practitioners alike for knowing more and more about less and less. Whatever the case, the firms and academic institutions we are part of need a mechanism that fosters the interdisciplinary research prerequisite to learning how to execute the marketing concept in environments of extensive and discontinuous change.

Even if this kind of research is not likely to emerge from current marketing departments, it seems to be arising as a natural momentum in an organization dedicated to bridging the academic and business marketing communities: the Marketing Science Institute.

This book, like so many other contributions to the store of marketing knowledge, would not be possible without MSI. Over the past decade, it has sponsored conferences and research integrating leading-edge marketing thought with information technology, anthropology, economics, finance, organizational behavior, and business strategy. Significantly, the impetus for this has come from marketing professionals themselves, who find MSI a congenial and responsive forum for interdisciplinary thinking. The evolutionary record of MSI research priorities demonstrates that the isolation and specialization of marketing does not describe the mindset of those marketers who gravitate into the orbit of this institution.

As it gets more difficult, and less interesting, to differentiate marketing from business problems, MSI is experiencing a rise in the number of company trustees without a classical marketing portfolio. For the same reason, there is a corresponding shift in the demographics of its academic researcher population. Because of the issues it focuses on, the leading thinkers it is consistently able to attract, its established infrastructure, and its 35-year track record as an effective bridge between the worlds of theory and practice, MSI is a prime candidate to become the intellectual Noah's ark that transports business professionals and academics, two by two, into their futures.

The authors in this book are intellectual heavyweights. Each has made significant individual contributions to the field over a sustained period. Many, during tenures as executive director of the Marketing Science Institute, exercised substantial influence over the direction and quality of breakthrough research.

But above all, each is a consummate scholar. It is this attribute that most distinguishes the pages that follow from other readings about what's happening and why. These authors gained their reputations from the quality of the research they conducted, from their ability to draw valid conclusions out of the data, and from the durability of their insights—rather than from an ability to concoct provocative speculation out of carefully culled anecdotes.

It has been my privilege over the past 20 years to work with and learn from each of them. It is now my privilege to commend this collection of their wisdom to everyone and anyone seriously interested in the futures of marketing and business. ■

Part I

➤ ➤ ➤ ➤ ➤ ➤ ➤

Trends

➤ 1

Janus and Marketing: The Past, Present, and Prospective Future of Marketing

Stephen A. Greyser

Not long ago, in an M.B.A. class at the Harvard Business School, I asked a student to describe how he thought Ralph Nader might react to a marketplace approach under discussion. "Who is Ralph Nader?" interjected another student. Indeed, *several* members of the class (mostly from outside the United States) didn't know who Nader was.

Why do I relate this story? Because every so often, in our discussions of where marketing is headed, I think we need to reflect on how it evolved to its present state. Such retrospection gives us permission—intellectually and perhaps psychologically—to look ahead and speculate about the future of marketing. Like the Roman god Janus, we gain perspective by looking both backward and forward.

In this regard, Professor Michael Baker of the University of Strathclyde in Scotland cogently observed: "Perhaps it is a symptom of advancing years that what is regarded as history by a new generation was an important element in the education and experience of the old" (1995, p. 1004). Likewise, my treatment here of the topic of marketing's future begins with reflections on its past.

"Getting to Now"

How did marketing develop? What eras passed in "getting to now"? In a 1960 *Journal of Marketing* article entitled "The Marketing Revolution," Robert Keith, then executive vice president of Pillsbury, offered trenchant insight.

Keith used Pillsbury's history as a metaphor for what he termed "the pattern of development in the marketing revolution" (p. 36). Keith crisply defined the focus on consumers as the center of what we call "the marketing concept." Keith said:

> "No longer is the company at the center of the business universe. Today the customer is at the center. Our attention has shifted from problems of production to problems of marketing, from the product we can make to the product the consumer wants us to make, from the company itself to the market place."

Pillsbury, he explained, had moved from a *production/manufacturing orientation* (where I characterize the key question for management as, "Can we make it?"), to a *sales orientation* ("Can we sell what we can make?"), to a *marketing orientation* ("Can we determine what consumers, or a group of consumers, want that we can make and sell profitably within our zones of skills?").

Of the first era of manufacturing, Keith wrote:

> "Our company philosophy in this era might have been stated this way: 'We are professional flour millers. Blessed with a supply of the finest North American wheat, plenty of water power, and excellent milling machinery, we produce flour of the highest quality. Our basic function is to mill high-quality flour, and of course (and almost incidentally) we must hire salesmen to sell it, just as we hire accountants to keep our books' " (p. 36).

In the second era, which for Pillsbury began in the 1930s, the company got closer to its channels and markets. Keith described the company's thinking during this period thus:

> "We are a flour-milling company, manufacturing a number of products for the consumer market. We must have a first-rate sales organization which can dispose of all the products we can make at a favorable price. We must back up this sales force with consumer advertising and market intelligence. We want our salesmen and our dealers to have all the tools they need for moving the output of our plants to the consumer" (p. 36).

The third era—one of marketing orientation—began in the 1940s with the company's successful R&D-based introduction of cake mixes:

> "We faced for the first time the necessity for selecting the best new products. We needed a set of criteria for selecting the kind of products we would manufacture. We needed an organization to establish and maintain these criteria, and for attaining maximum sale of the products we did select.

> "We needed, in fact, to build into our company a new management function which would direct and control all the other corporate functions from procurement to production to advertising to sales. This function was marketing. Our solution was to establish the present marketing department.

> "This department developed the criteria which we would use in determining which products to market. *And these criteria were, and are, nothing more nor less than those of the consumer herself.*

> "If we were to restate our philosophy during [this period] as simply as possible, it would read: 'We make and sell products for consumers' " (p. 37).

In short, Keith had traversed a route to what I term "getting to now." He went on to predict:

> "Marketing will become the basic motivating force for the entire corporation. Soon it will be true that every activity of the corporation—from finance to sales to production—is aimed at satisfying the needs and desires of the consumer. When that stage of development is reached, the marketing revolution will be complete" (p. 38).

In recent years we have witnessed yet another era, an era oriented to consumer/customer satisfaction (both household consumers and business-to-business customers). Now the challenge is, Can we generate continuing business (i.e., loyalty purchasing) via consumer/customer satisfaction with what—and how—we make, sell, and service? In short, can we provide meaningful continuing relationship purchasing through what we market and the process of how we go about it? The strong interest in recent years in loyalty-building marketing and in customer satisfaction lends support to the arrival of this "new era."

What will come next? Perhaps an era of consumer welfare.[1] This will occur when marketing not only provides satisfaction to us as consumers/customers—but also passes the test of serving us as *citizens*. Consider, for instance, the "green marketing" of environmentally friendly products, the "lean marketing" of healthy/nutritious food products, and the spate of initiatives antipathetic to marketing products—such as tobacco and alcohol—considered inimical to our health.

Let me take us back in time again, and explore further the advent of the marketing concept.

---

1. *Philip Kotler and I have independently written about this phenomenon.*

The Marketing Concept

When and how did the consumer become the focal point for marketing philosophy and practice? Bernard LaLonde has carefully delved into the origins of this phenomenon, and has traced it to the 1920s (LaLonde 1964). However, most scholars locate the first articulation of the marketing concept at General Electric, with Vice President Jack McKitterick. An early allusion to customer focus appeared in the company's 1952 annual report, and in 1957, at an American Marketing Association meeting, McKitterick gave fuller voice to the idea. As originally described, GE "introduces the marketing [executive] at the beginning rather than the end of the production cycle, and . . . integrate[s] marketing into each phase." McKitterick underscored the role, and goal, for marketing: "the principal task of . . . marketing . . . is not so much to be skillful in making the customer do what suits the interests of the business as to be skillful in conceiving and then making the business do what suits the interest of the customer" (McKitterick 1957, p. 78).

Also during the 1950s, respected thinkers such as Peter Drucker, Theodore Levitt, and Philip Kotler gave added stimulus to broadening management knowledge of (and appreciation for) marketing. They put marketing squarely at the center of business (and even non-business) organizations. In 1954 Peter Drucker's pioneering observations offered a seminal perspective on marketing as the key differentiator between business and other human organizations. Marketing, he suggested, "is the whole business seen from the point of view of its final result, that is, from the customer's point of view" (1954, p. 39). Drucker further notes that "the customer . . . determines what a business is . . . [and] is the foundation of a business" (p. 37).

In Theodore Levitt's classic, "Marketing Myopia," he outlined the proper practice of marketing: "Selling is not marketing. Selling concerns itself with the tricks and techniques of getting people to exchange their cash for your product. It is not concerned with the values that the exchange is all about. And it does not, as marketing invariably does, view the entire business process as consisting of a tightly integrated effort to discover, create, arouse, and satisfy customer needs" (1960, p. 55).

In 1969, Philip Kotler and Sidney Levy extended marketing's central role to *all* kinds of organizations, business and nonbusiness, through "the broadening of the concept of marketing" (1969). Three years later, to reaffirm the point, Kotler advanced "a generic concept of marketing" (1972). He explained that marketing occurs when there are two or more social units, of which at least one (the marketer) seeks a response from the other (the market) regarding a product, idea, or behavior.

Over time, the pivotal role of consumers/customers has become the widely accepted central tenet of marketing thought and action. "Understanding consumers/customers" typically launches marketing textbooks, and the issue of consumer targets and of how a product or service will satisfy buying motives is an essential component of any planned marketing program. Numerous business and academic authorities have elaborated on the subject. I characterize the salience of consumers/customers thus: "consumers: the alpha and omega of marketing."

The Practice of Marketing

Thus far I have concentrated on the philosophy of marketing. What about the "doing" of marketing, i.e., specific marketing plans and programs?

Two key constructs warrant mention in this regard. One is the *marketing mix*, an idea developed by Neil Borden in the 1940s. Borden spelled out a taxonomy of the tools of marketing ("elements of the mix") to be employed in marketing programs in varying ways, but within a coherent overall approach (1964). Foreshadowing more recent considerations, Borden included outside forces such as government and ethical issues as components of the mix.

The second idea underpinning marketing programs is the *"four Ps."* Popularized by E. Jerome McCarthy in his widely adopted textbook, this guide to developing marketing programs posited product, price, promotion (communications and selling), and place (i.e., distribution) as central considerations of any marketing program (1960).

More recently, marketing strategy and programs are described as *adding value* for consumers/customers. Indeed, some of that value-adding is now coming *from* consumers and customers rather than solely from the company. We see this phenomenon first in the birth of consumer and marketing research. In the 1970s, the development of consumer affairs offices brought consumer/customer interest several steps closer. Now, through such vehicles as user panels that help design and configure a firm's product and service patterns, consumers/customers can add value to companies' abilities to add value!

Power and Influence in the Marketplace

The recognition of the primacy of consumers has led to change in another important aspect of the marketplace: the *interface* between marketers and consumers, especially regarding power and influence. In "Marketing Myopia," despite his core message, Levitt himself referred to selling as operating with a view that "the customer is someone out there who, with proper cunning, can be separated from his or her money" (1960, p. 55).

Vance Packard's 1957 best-seller, *The Hidden Persuaders*, and other antimarketing tomes underscored this perspective. Even as early as the 1930s, with Kallett and Schlink's *One Hundred Million Guinea Pigs* and the onset of the Depression, the motives of marketing and advertising came under close scrutiny. In the 1960s, a surge of antimarketing feeling was accompanied by the growth of consumerism and regulatory initiatives.

The late Raymond A. Bauer and I offered a tripartite analysis of the marketplace relationship between marketers and consumers. The three models—alternative conceptions of the marketplace—we dubbed *manipulative* (a critic's model), *service* (a probusiness model), and *transactional* (our exchange-based model, derived dominantly from communications research, that portrays the market in a more give-and-take fashion)(see Bauer and Greyser 1967 and Greyser 1972). Each model employs different assumptions about the power balance in the marketplace, the origin of consumer needs and desires, the type of consumer power exercised, the "warning" to consumers and/or business that permeates the marketplace, and the role of the marketer. The accompanying chart (Figure 1), developed by Dr. Cheryl Owens and myself, elucidates the models.

Let me note that Richard Bagozzi has also been an articulate advocate of "marketing as exchange," most notably in his 1975 *Journal of Marketing* article by that title.

Other Developments

This retrospective of the development of marketing prompts some additional observations. One is the *constancy of change*: there is virtually no period since World War I in which marketing institutions and practice were not changing in important ways. Consider, for example, the reduced significance of agricultural commodities (as a result of processed foods) or the decline of wholesaling (and rise of multifarious distribution avenues). These alone have produced significant changes in marketing practice.

At the same time, great strides have been made in applying disciplinary knowledge and in developing and using advanced analytic techniques. Since the 1950s, one can track significant developments in marketing knowledge and application in discipline-based theories, managerial frameworks and approaches, models and measurement, and research methods and statistical techniques.[2]

---

2. *See for example, Chapter 3 in Myers, Massy, and Greyser (1980), in which this structure is employed.*

Figure 1. Comparing and Contrasting the Three Models

Models Assumption About. . .	The Manipulative Model	The Transactional Model	The Service Model
Power Balance in the Marketplace	Marketers Dominate	Consumer-Marketer Balance	Consumers Dominate
Origin of Consumer Needs/Desires	With Marketers	With Consumers and Marketers	With Consumers
Type of Consumer Power	Forced Consumer Choice	Consumer Choice	Consumer Sovereignty
Marketplace Warning	Caveat Emptor	Caveat Omnes	Caveat Venditor
Role of Marketer	To Persuade/Seduce Consumers The Consumer's Adversary	To Work with Consumers The Consumer's Partner	To Service/Cater to Consumers The Consumer's Servant

Marketing Science Institute's Impacts

In reviewing and interpreting changes in the philosophy, practice, and role of marketing, we should also note the impacts of the Marketing Science Institute. Since its founding in 1961, MSI has affected these aspects of marketing through its research programs and projects, particularly via its research priorities initiatives of the past 20-plus years. Perhaps most significantly, MSI's contributions derive from its institutional commitment to serving as a *bridge* between business and academe, its recognition that practice can inform—even lead—academic thinking and research, and its accompanying belief in the efficacy of promoting knowledge that is relevant.

A principal "driver" of MSI's structural ability to make such contributions is the Research Priorities Program, which increasingly influences academic research agendas for many marketing faculty in the United States and around the world. For those who are unfamiliar with the origins of the program, it was undertaken in 1974 as a way to search for the MSI equivalent of the "most-wanted" list of topics member companies considered most desirable for meaningful research. Of interest is that the topic judged the single highest priority item in that first year was "Managing New Product Development and Introduction." (This led to the work of Edgar Pessemier, who came to MSI as visiting research professor in 1974-75; by the way, some 20 years later, new product development was identified as the most important research priority in MSI's 1992 and 1994 biennial research priorities processes!) Research on consumer goods promotion and the landmark Churchill-Ford-Walker research on industrial salesforce management also emerged from that initial 1974 research priorities process.

In the mid-1980s, Paul Bloom carefully and comprehensively chronicled and analyzed the impacts of MSI's research for the book *Knowledge Development in Marketing: The MSI Experience.* The breadth of marketing territory experiencing positive effects encompassed strategic marketing, industrial marketing, services marketing (a field where MSI pioneered organized research), consumer behavior, advertising and mass communications, sales promotion, research methodology and model building, and marketing and public policy. Were a sequel to be done now, brand equity would be added to the fields where MSI's research has helped shape academic thinking and influence practice.

"Migrated Marketing": The Next Age

In this commentary, I have sought to address how we have "gotten to now" in terms of marketing philosophy and marketing practice.

The recognition of the salience of the consumer and the centrality of marketing itself have over time inevitably led to a much broader understanding of and knowledge about marketing on the part of *non*marketing executives. Further, the emergence and gradual acceptance of these two key ideas have had profound implications organizationally.

In the mid-1990s, the very act of putting the consumer at the top of the organization chart, or at the center of company/brand planning and programs, has caused all the nonmarketing functional parts/people in the management group to consider and learn about consumers. Thus, with consumers and marketing linked at the very core of business enterprise, nonmarketing people have had to devote meaningful attention to the process of marketing strategy and planning. In essence, nonmarketing executives had to become more marketing oriented.

With the passage of time—and with university programs, executive education sessions, and the patient instruction of marketing colleagues—a generation of businesspeople have grasped marketing principles, even if they do not carry formal marketing responsibility. This phenomenon I term *"migrated marketing."*

Indeed, in today's fast-paced world, the tasks of building and maintaining a consumer-oriented entity, and of helping an entire organization become marketing-minded, are vital. In fact, these jobs are so important that they transcend the marketing department itself. While the marketing function ("doing marketing") belongs to the marketing department, becoming and being marketing-minded is *everybody's* job.

What happens when (almost) everybody *is* doing that job? As companies have become more marketing-minded, there have been substantial reductions in the formal "marketing departments" which *do* marketing. In short, a corollary of the trend to better organizational *thinking* about marketing is the dispersion of the *activity* of marketing, e.g., via task forces.

What I see is a simultaneous *upgrading of orientation and downsizing of formal function.* In this age of migrated marketing, marketing-mindedness is permeating the organization—a noninvidious "metasta-sized marketing." Will this mean the elimination of the marketing department? I doubt it. However, I would suggest that the downsizing of marketing departments is not transitory. When package-goods delivery people effectively perform front-line sales and service functions, when hotel or airline check-in staff are the first line of a truly customer-friendly atmosphere, when an integrated development task force supplants official departmental representatives—then formal marketing department staffs can be smaller, even as marketing's operational effect is bigger.

Others contributing to this volume will explore further implications, for practice and for teaching, of the changes I have cited. Some of them may offer alternative scenarios of the future. I trust that my observations and comments will help inform those perspectives—and the reader's. ■

➤ 2

Looking Ahead at the Marketplace; It's Global and It's Changing

John U. Farley

"Let's look at the U.S. telecommunications market. . . ."

"You mean the U.S. segment of the world telecommunications market, don't you?"

　　—Exchange with Bell Labs engineer at 1976 executive program

The task the contributors to this volume were charged with was to consider the future of marketing over the last few years of this decade and the first few of the next. It's hard to do this without some attention to likely changes in the markets themselves that will have a major effect on the way that corporations manage marketing. For large corporations domiciled in the United States, such changes may be particularly important as they are likely to occur outside their areas of strength.

I am not going to try to go into detail about what the futurists are predicting during this period, although it is important to remember how quickly things change. The *New York Times* on November 8, 1988 (just seven years before we gave our first presentations on these papers at the MSI Trustees meeting in the fall of 1995), contained, among others, the following stories: George Bush, having soundly defeated Michael Dukakis, appointed James Baker secretary of state.

The Dow stood at 2200, with technical reasons for thinking it would not go much higher. The Soviet Army threatened the Baltic countries, demanding that they forget any possibility of independence. The New York Giants (7 wins, 2 losses) had just beaten the Dallas Cowboys (2 wins, 7 losses) to gain first place in the standings, etc. . . .

I am going to take the liberty of applying a somewhat personal spin on the following questions:

> ➤ Where will market growth come from?

> ➤ What will large companies, particularly those used to concentrating on large home markets, have to do to respond to changes in their traditional patterns of search for growth?

The quote that opens this chapter is from an exchange in a program designed to help highly qualified engineers become more market oriented—an issue that still has currency 20 years later. It is the usual situation of student teaching teacher, and I owe that anonymous student a lot. After that day in 1976, my thinking about the American market has always been placed, as it should be, in the context of a corresponding world market. It has turned out to be easy to think this way about markets; during the ensuing two decades, I have seldom run across any market that did not have both major international customers and competitors, or at least a very real but unrealized potential for both.

Marketing's Role: The Search for Growth

"The complex of factors most consistently related to higher profits (present and future) blends environment, strategy and organization rationally in a planned and deliberate way:

> ➤ Competing in rapidly growing markets

> ➤ Securing high market shares in national markets around the globe (supported by production in

many locales) through innovation secured by product development and an entrepreneurial organizational style"

—From *Toward an Integrative Explanation of Corporate Financial Performance*, Noel Capon, John U. Farley, and Scott Hoenig, 1996

My guess is that marketing's most important role in the next decade will involve the search for growing markets. My favorite definition for the role of marketing in the firm has always been creation of value for buyers and capture of a significant part of that created value. There is solid evidence that participation in growing markets is probably the best long-run way to create value and gain higher-than-average profits (Capon, Farley, and Hoenig 1996, quoted above), and the search for growth is now a truly global business. Cost containment and downsizing, while important and possibly effective in the short run, have limits in terms of renewability. Participation in growing markets does not.

A firm that maintains a continuous record of higher-than-average revenue growth is probably also engaged in continuous introduction of new products, opening of new markets, or both (Capon, Farley, Lehmann, and Hulbert 1992). Even if that growth comes primarily through acquisition, the acquirees generally are expected to provide market growth.

Organizations can certainly create conditions that raise the likelihood of higher financial returns, and MSI has played a leadership role in sponsoring research on these conditions (Deshpandé, Farley, and Webster 1993, 1996). For example, organizational cultures and climates that stress entrepreneurship and external orientation no doubt help foster sales growth. However, the fundamental likelihood is that over the next decade, many firms will focus attention away from markets that are just big and towards markets that promise higher-than-average growth.

The Markets to Be

"Everyone in Kuala Lumpur is rich enough to have a maid.
But no one in Kuala Lumpur wants to be a maid."
—Malaysian M.B.A. student at Columbia circa 1985

There seems to be a consensus that better-than-average growth of
profits depends to a very large degree on new sales from markets that
are experiencing better-than-average growth. Over the past couple of
decades, economic growth in the nonindustrial world has snuck up
behind many American companies. The major driving force has simply been differential compound GNP growth rates (see Table 1),
which have slowly edged (rather than propelled) many individual
economies into relative prosperity. Of course, the short-term impact
of a few years of 10 percent or even 5 percent growth grabs headlines,
but overall it has been a race involving relative speeds of tortoises
rather than of tortoises versus hares. A good deal of this growth has
been concentrated in Asia, for reasons that, as a contemporary matter,
are not wholly clear. For instance, Korea in three decades has moved
from one of the poorest countries in the world to one of the richest;
theories as to why abound. Of the industrial countries, Japan has realized by far the greatest growth. Relative growth rates are not expected
to change materially, although there will no doubt continue to be better and worse years. For example, I lived in Singapore in the 1980s
during a year that both Singapore and Malaysian officials were wor-
ried because they anticipated only a 5 percent income growth.

The Western industrial countries have, of course, grown economi-
cally as well during this same period, but there seems to be an
American corporate litany that foresees disproportionate growth and
profit gain outside the North American market. Europe is not growing any faster than North America, and European firms are also seeking above-average growth. As a result, everyone's attention must and
will necessarily turn to markets outside the traditional industrial

(roughly the 28-member Organization for Economic Cooperation and Development [OECD]) world.

More important, most projections over our time frame call for more of the same in the near and middle future (Table 2).

Table 1. Long-term Income Growth for a Sample of Countries (U.S. $)

| | Gross National Product | | | |
| | Per Capita | | Growth | |
	1973	1993	As % of 1973	Average Annual Rate
Low-income Developing World				
Bangladesh	80	220	175	8.75
Kenya	200	270	35	1.75
Middle-income Industrial World				
Thailand	270	2,110	681	34.05
Malaysia	600	3,140	423	21.15
Brazil	760	2,930	286	
New Industrial World				
Singapore	1,710	19,850	1,061	53.05
Korea	430	7,660	1,681	84.05
Resource-rich World				
Saudi Arabia	2,130	7,810[a]	267	14.05
Kuwait	4,580	19,360	323	16.15
Industrial World				
France	4,580	22,490	391	19.55
U.S.	6,910	24,740	258	12.90
Japan	3,470	31,490	807	40.35
U.S. Consumer Price Index	39	127	226	11.30
U.S. GDP Deflator	42	123	193	9.65

[a]1992

Source: World Tables 1995, *Published for the World Bank, Johns Hopkins University Press, Baltimore, MD*

Table 2. Projected Mean GNP Growth to 2000

World	3.0%
Developed Market Economies	
North America	+2.7%
Developed East (esp. Japan)	+3.0%
European Community	+2.4%
Rest	+2.1%
Eastern Europe	+3.0% (after 1997)
Southeast Asia	+6.3%
Latin America	+3.9%
Africa	+3.4% (per capita 0.4%)

Source: Adapted from Project LINK

Big and Growing Are Not the Same

"We look at the American market as big but as not particularly profitable."

—Japanese M.B.A. student sponsored at Wharton by his firm, 1993

In the late 1980s, a firm with which I was associated conducted some research on what European managers anticipated to be the greatest benefits from the 1992 integration of the European Economic Community. We were sure that their responses would focus on cost savings related to easier flows of information and goods across within-market boundaries. To our surprise, the number one benefit, as seen through the eyes of managers of large European enterprises, was that rationalization would help them compete more effectively against American firms in Europe. Second most important was the ability to compete more effectively in the American market itself. This perspective has bearings on the strategic value of home markets in the industrial countries.

The Big Markets

There is no doubt that the big markets are in the industrial world, and the OECD slightly expanded to include the Asian Newly Industrialized Countries (NICs) is a good approximation. The U.S. market is generally biggest, often in the range of 20 percent of the world market. The Japanese market, generally about half as big, is second, followed by Germany and then a group including France, Britain, etc. The international strategy of any firm, wherever it is headquartered, will take account of these countries. While their markets for new products or services will continue to grow relatively quickly, the economies themselves are growing relatively slowly. Furthermore, the major world-class competitors in most industries are generally located in these same countries, so a U.S. firm's foreign market in Germany is a German firm's domestic market.

As for the U.S. domestic market itself, there is nothing wrong per se with a decision by an American company to focus on the American market. Life for Americans is quieter there, and there is no need for management to disrupt family life with time abroad. However, it is important, in making such a decision, to pay attention to how foreign competitors perceive the American market and what they expect from it, as illustrated in the quote above. Given its size and openness, the American market is likely to be a key part of the strategy of virtually any company with any significant international operation, wherever home base may be.

The Understated Markets

It is a good idea to check income figures other than those from conventional national accounts—especially for markets that are growing particularly fast. For example, purchasing power parity estimates of the Vietnamese market indicate that per capita income is more than double, perhaps four times, that indicated by GDP (U.S. $250). A couple of days in Shanghai will convince you that the same is true of China.

The international economic sector will probably continue to out-grow the domestic. Even for the relatively mature markets, econometric forecasts of international trade to the end of the century indicate that imports and exports will grow at rates well above the rates of basic economic growth (Table 3). Imports and exports are, of course, only part of the puzzle, and not necessarily the most profit generating; direct investment is probably the best route to above-average returns internationally (Capon, Farley, and Hoenig 1996). The fact that U.S. direct investments in foreign plant and equipment are now larger than those of any other country is a cause for optimism, but there is no guarantee that this trend will continue.

Table 3. Projected Growth Rates of Industrial Imports and Exports

	Mean Annual Growth to Year 2000	
	Imports	**Exports**
World		8.6%
Developed Market Economies	7.0%	7.1%
Developing Economies	12.9%	12.5%
in: Latin America	8.8%	8.0%
Southeast Asia	15.2%	15.3%
China	15.4%	14.1%
C.I.S. and Baltic Republics (after 1997)	8.0%	8.1%

Source: Adapted from Project LINK

The Numbers Are Important Too

"If we could only sell one piece every year to every Chinese. . . ."
—CEO of major U.S. consumer goods producer, 1994

The basic fact remains that the industrial world is far outnumbered in terms of total world population. India and China alone contribute 2 billion of the nearly 6 billion people—to be 10 billion not long after the turn of the century. Figure 1 shows the overall population figures for 1990 and estimated for the year 2000, and Table 4 is a reminder of how many really big countries are now outside the industrial world. I am afraid that too many Americans of my generation, still influenced by conditions after World War II, have not come to grips with the realities of economic and demographic development in the last generation. I still run into people who lump together the nonindustrial world as "underdeveloped countries." As we enter the 21st century, most truly underdeveloped countries are in Central Africa, and most other nonindustrial countries should be classified as industrializing. The current argument over whether China should be classified as an industrial country for entry into the World Trade Organization has substance as well as form.

There are three basic elements of demography that will remain constant during the time span that we are considering, and that have direct bearing on marketing:

1. Total population will continue to grow at about 2 percent, almost all outside of the industrial world. Unfortunately for Africa, population growth will continue to wipe out economic growth at the per capita level. Economies virtually everywhere else are growing faster than populations.

2. The cities outside the industrial world will grow at three times the rate of overall population, creating pockets of very rapidly growing, money-based markets in virtually

every country in the world. In fact, of the world's 25 largest cities, only a half dozen are in the industrial world. The largest is Mexico City, and Brazil alone has a dozen cities with populations of a million people. Market researchers estimate that China has 100—yes, one hundred—cities with populations above 1 million.

3. The age disparities between the industrial and nonindustrial worlds will continue, with average ages in the industrial world about double (going on 40) the average ages in the developing world. If you sell things that appeal to oldsters, or that they need whether they like it or not, the growth is in the industrial world. If you depend on family formation and younger markets, best plan to look elsewhere.

Figure 1. World Population: 1990 vs. 2000

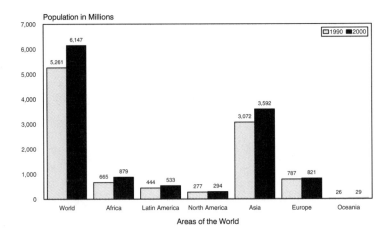

Source: World Bank, World Population Projections, 1990

Table 4. Markets: The Numbers

Populations	"Nonindustrial" Countries	"Industrial" Countries
100+ Million	China Indonesia Nigeria India Brazil Bangladesh Pakistan	U.S.A. C.I.S. Japan
45-100 Million	Egypt Mexico Thailand Turkey Philippines Korea Vietnam	Germany France Italy U.K.
10 Million	80+ Countries	Austria Belgium Norway Sweden, etc.

Which Countries and Which Markets?

There is a kind of inexorable logic in the geography of international marketing strategies. There are somewhere between 150 and 200 "countries" or at least more or less independent decision-making entities, and the U.N. has about 160 members. Most genuine multinationals have markets of some significance in a little over 100 countries, with direct representation, depending to some extent on the industry, in perhaps a third of these. The industrial countries represent the vast majority of sales (but not necessarily growth or potential growth) in most businesses, with the G7 countries representing the majority of these. Probably more important than sales, the G7 holds the majority of the world's investments.

Twice over the past 20 years I have had the occasion to rank the most important industrializing countries. I have taken this to mean countries with large populations providing a good base for potential markets (particularly industrial markets), large economies with unrealized potential for growth, and which exert large economic leverage on the region. The list of my top five hasn't changed very much; I thought that I'd add my projection to 2003 as well:

1973	1993	2003
Brazil	China	India
Nigeria	Indonesia	China
India	Brazil	Brazil
China	India	Indonesia
Indonesia	Nigeria	Nigeria

This does not deny the enormous returns in particular countries, for example, to those who established early positions in the 1970s and 1980s in Asia's four NICs (Korea, Taiwan, Singapore, Hong Kong), nor similar returns for more recent investment in Malaysia or Thailand. Vietnam, with a population of 75 million and sustained near double-digit economic growth, is close to joining its wealthier neighbors. However, in these cases, the surviving early investor reaped the greatest gains, the process of investment was a long and tedious one, and there was limited leverage to other markets of the sort that the five countries listed above promise.

As to specific product and service markets with the greatest growth potential, there is no clear pattern in the futurists' predictions about whole sectors that can be expected to realize sustained worldwide compound growth over the decade of 5 or 6 percent. Best candidates seem to be: health care, particularly for the aging; information management products, particularly software; and leisure time industries. The last have caught on much faster than was anticipated, even in workaholic but newly rich Asia.

Macroeconomics Giveth and Macroeconomics Can Take Away

"This Sukhothai is good.
In the water, there is fish; in the fields, there is rice.
The King takes no advantage of the people.
Whoever wants to trade, trades.
The faces of the people shine bright with happiness."

—Inscription on a stone in Sukhothai, the ancient kingdom of Siam in the 12th and 13th centuries A.D.

Many people—Americans and others—automatically associate international business and high risk. It may be that individual losses abroad are more visible or at least more newsworthy than their counterparts. Our research has in fact shown the contrary—that American manufacturers with high fractions of sales generated outside of North America not only have higher average rates of return on capital, but they also have less over-time variability in profits (at least one proxy for measuring risk) than those firms with a high proportion of domestic revenues (Capon, Farley, and Hulbert 1988; Capon, Farley, and Hoenig 1996).

This is not to say that there are not risks and genuine losses associated, for example, with the epidemic of ethnic conflicts that seems to circle the globe. Avoiding them when possible and escaping early when caught is good management, but managing these sorts of idiosyncratic risks is already factored into the profitability figures mentioned above.

However, there are some classes of risk, mostly involving macroeconomics, that transcend boundaries. In 1980 or maybe even in 1990, I would never have dared to predict: (1) that there would be almost universal acknowledgment that policies of complex economic interdependencies among countries are desirable, and (2) that conservative macroeconomic policies within countries should be pursued.

The demise of the Soviet Union removed the final intellectual support from alternative approaches, such as import substitution which has dominated macroeconomics in Brazil and India and has had wide influence in many other countries. The expansion of international trade from U.S.$200 million to U.S.$4 trillion over the past two decades has been firmly based on this macroeconomic foundation, and the glitches during that period (the Latin American debt crisis, for example) can largely be traced to deviation from these macroeconomic principles. As the Sukhothai inscription above indicates, this sort of macroeconomics has been known to work for a long time. Sukhothai was, of course, neither a democracy nor an open-market system—neither are really required for a functioning noncommand economic system to work.

The macroeconomic risk is that significant parts of the world might return to some form of mercantilism. There are large numbers of temporarily powerless opponents of the current macroeconomic environment who stand ready at a moment's notice to return economies to the order and discipline of command status or at least of import substitution. Despite the eclipse of Russia as a philosophical center for command economics, it is not clear that the nations of the former Soviet Union are paying much more than lip service to reform in the macroeconomic sphere. The transition for India has not been and will not be an easy one. Recent protests of Philippine workers against cheap imports show that problems of the most unexpected sorts can crop up in the most unexpected places.

It is, incidentally, much to the credit of the United States that its consistent pursuit, over nearly five decades, of a foreign policy based on creating economic interdependencies among nations has succeeded and has, at least for the time being, formed the basis for an extended period of relative peace and economic liberalization among nation states.

At the same time, it is very discouraging that a new generation of conflict not drawn along the lines of nation states has flared up to replace the old kinds of military conflict to which U.S. policy was directed. We might be somewhat hopeful that economic integration across nation states can have some positive effect on this new brand of conflict, but only time will tell us.

Globalization Strategy – Round 2?

此乃宜家傢俬店內專用目錄，
用後請歸還出口處，多謝合作。

— Quote from the IKEA catalogue in Hong Kong showroom

A decade ago, a debate rose up over whether markets had become so homogeneous that universal or global strategies were not only practical but necessary to take advantage of production economies. The irrepressible Theodore Levitt (1983) took the null "aye" position in one of his periodic *Harvard Business Review* best-sellers, "The Globalization of Markets." The "nay" position was much more amorphous, ranging from an almost global position to pure "every country and culture is different" alternative hypotheses. The debate was lively, very visible, but was inconclusive. Examples were the usual suspects—Parker Pens' unsuccessful strategy for the nays to Coca-Cola and McDonald's successes for the ayes.

Since then, a variety of ventures much more identifiable to a particular culture have realized remarkable international expansion with relatively minor modification of an identifiably culture-based strategy. An excellent example is IKEA showrooms, built solidly on Swedish blue and yellow, housing furniture with solidly old Norse names, and sold as packaged products to be picked up in private cars at shopping centers. After languishing through a couple of decades of Scandinavian success, expansion began into 24 countries. An estimated 100 million people will visit the IKEA showrooms this year. In Hong Kong, a relatively carless society, the same unassembled furniture with the same ancient Scandinavian names is sold through outlets with the same distinctively Swedish layout. (The above text is the familiar, "This is an IKEA in-Store Catalogue, please return at exit after use. Thank you." [*sic*])

I believe that, as John Little of MIT would say, globalization is an idea whose time has come in a special sense: it is time for some careful research on

1. why the highly visible global successes have worked,

2. perhaps more important, why the highly invisible failures have not, and

3. how to tell the difference beforehand and identify good candidates for globalization.

It is important that this work stay away from multiple cause explanations based on single cases, which seemed to characterize much of the Levitt round of debate on globalization.

Marketing and Culture

> "I felt as if someone had walked into my living room with their shoes on."
>> —Reaction of Japanese woman member of a focus group shown a reel of American TV commercials. Quoted by George Fields (1983), *From Bonzai to Levis*

> "Western co-authors are useful because it is easier for them to think linearly."
>> —Comment of an Asian marketing scholar, 1989

It adds very little to dialogue on international markets to point out that a foreign marketer must be particularly attuned to local culture in order to avoid mistakes that would simply not be made by a local competitor who instinctively understands the local culture. In fact, the basic reason that culture is so hard to understand is that it is often impossible for members of a culture to articulate why they do a particular thing in a particular way. Cultural gaffes make good reading; each of us, I am sure, thinks that he or she would not have made any of the published classic mistakes, even though each was made by an experienced and thinking manager.

However, it appears to me that there is a more basic and fundamental problem that now deserves the attention of marketers, particularly American—possible cultural characteristics of marketing itself. It is more than a curiosity that about half of the media advertising done on the globe is done in the United States. It may very well be true that advertising in particular and marketing in general simply "takes" better in the United States than it does elsewhere. The word "marketing" does not translate very well into other languages (the French use "le marketing," for example), while the closest French words don't grasp the basic idea or are even slightly pejorative ("commercialization" and "vulgarization" in French, for example). You can make a strong case that marketing itself has a strong cultural context which is primarily Western and heavily American. America is, of course, widely admired around the world, but that does not guarantee that marketing is a technology that will transfer readily—particularly into economies in which distribution dominates the other three Ps of the marketing mix.

This is a phenomenon not related to nation state but to cultural history of groups of people. For example, we have some evidence (Tan and Farley 1987) that cultures steeped in Confucian and Buddhist values react quite differently than those based in Western values to advertising—not necessarily negatively, but just differently. A very large part of the market growth potential described earlier is in such cultures. There is a very large block of countries with a partially common cultural background and about which we have very limited knowledge concerning the role of marketing—the Islamic states, of which there are about 50. While there are great differences across, as well as within, these countries, the Islamic states represent the largest single group of culture-linked countries in the world. Their population is about double that of the industrial world, and their profiles are in general like those described earlier—relatively young, growing populations with low but relatively rapidly growing incomes. In addition to the ubiquitous advice to understand market culture, I suggest that we need to take steps to understand the cultural characteristics of marketing management as it is now practiced, and how these characteristics interact with various basic cultural perceptions and values.

Impediments

"We have had the number one brand in the U.S. market for 20 years, and we still don't understand the American consumer."

—Chief strategic planner (completely bilingual in English) of a European multinational manufacturer, 1990

"They keep sending me people who speak French but don't understand a thing about doing business in France."

—Senior French executive of European operations of an American multinational, 1991

In the mid-1980s, I served as executive director of MSI. Perhaps my biggest surprise was how much time we spent at workshops and conferences talking not about markets but about organizations. Again and again, discussions turned to dealing with how a company can avoid standing in its own way in getting products out and into promising markets. My observation is that MSI meetings I have attended since that time have been, if anything, more concerned with such issues.

Most of the impediments to success in international markets have to do with who will get the benefits of the growth I described earlier, rather than with whether the growth will occur.

Certainly, international organizations of many businesses are changing rapidly. Unfortunately, we don't have a very good research-based idea about what organizational forms are most closely linked to profitability (Capon, Farley, and Hoenig 1996; Farley and Kobrin 1995). We do have some cross-national evidence that organizational forms, and particularly organizational cultures, relatively open to market signals and entrepreneurial ideas function well in a variety of cultural settings, while hierarchies and inward-looking firm cultures perform less well (Deshpandé, Farley, and Webster 1996).

Managers often ask us to name companies who "do it right" so they can be copied in terms of international organization. There is clearly considerable uncertainty even among successful companies about international organization. Our research indicates that some companies do more things a little better and prosper as a result, but that no single company stands out as having gotten organization right once and for all (Capon, Farley, and Hoenig 1996). My personal view, and it must be treated as just that, is that successful multinational firms with very small home markets have been more innovative in terms of their international organizations, and it may be wise to watch them for signals about what will work best. However, it is genuinely dangerous for an organization to try to copy form from another without attention to the relevance of that form to their own organizational culture (Deshpandé, Farley, and Webster 1993, 1996).

Summing Up

The general themes I have raised in this rather personal look at marketing's world over the next decade or so are, of course, couched in a web of extraordinary complexity for the individual manager and organization—particularly for American organizations used to feasting on a large, dependable, and growing domestic market which has historically been more profitable than it is currently. It is not easy to do business abroad, and there is every reason to believe that foreign competitors will continue to do everything possible to make it harder. Internally for most firms, it is hard to deflect attention from market size (where the revenues have come from in the past) to market growth (where increased profitability will come from in five years or a decade). Changes in the environment often mandate changes in the organization, and large industrial bureaucracies are not necessarily society's most effective agents of change. I would suggest the following food for thought for the next decade:

1. Market growth, particularly profitable market growth, will occur disproportionately outside of the currently industrialized world. During the period, demographic aging will work against industrial countries on both the demand and production sides of many established industries, as domestic market growth slows and as the proportion of young workers and buyers in the population shrinks.

2. Real product/service innovation and attendant rapid market growth seem to provide the most dependable route to above-average profitability in the next decade. Shortening product life cycles, which speed up even further as a market spreads internationally, pay a premium to timing and coordination during introduction and early growth of a market. MSI research has shown uncertainty as to whether it is a good idea to be first into a new and growing market (Nakata and Sivakumar 1995), but there is little debate that it is a poor idea to be last.

3. International business is not risky per se, and the variability of earnings of successful international companies is in fact lower than average. The real risks are macroeconomic and cultural, rather than political.

4. We need a much better idea about how culture and modern practices of marketing, which were basically developed in a handful of Western countries, interact.

5. Firms with very large home markets are most likely to make marketing mistakes internationally.

6. International organizations are changing rapidly, and multinational firms with very small home markets seem to be the most innovative organizationally. There is, however, considerable uncertainly about what kind of international organization is "best." It is important for American firms, coming from a culture not attuned to investment in foreign languages, to notice the key role of languages in the functioning of these organizations. English alone will no longer do.

7. It is a good idea to remember that managers who made the decisions that produced the classic international marketing gaffes (silly or obscene brand names, culturally inappropriate products, etc.) were generally neither stupid nor unaware. They simply lacked the breadth and depth of knowledge required to function well in international markets. ■

Part II

➤ ➤ ➤ ➤ ➤ ➤ ➤

Organizational Responses and Implications

➤ 3

The Future Role of Marketing in the Organization

Frederick E. Webster, Jr.

Among the several management functions, marketing has the most difficulty defining its position in the organization because it is simultaneously culture, strategy, and tactics. As *organizational culture*, it is expressed in the "marketing concept" (Drucker 1954; Keith 1960; McKitterick 1957) as a set of values and beliefs driving the organization, a fundamental commitment to serving customers' needs as the path to sustained profitability. As *strategy*, marketing helps the firm respond to a changing market environment by defining market segments, selecting the segments that the company will serve, and developing and positioning product offerings for those target markets. As *tactics*, marketing is seen in the day-to-day activities of product management, pricing, distribution, and marketing communications such as advertising, personal selling, and sales promotion.

In the last decade of the 20th century, traditional forms of business organization have been subject to intense scrutiny. The result is a process of transformation of lasting impact. Tight hierarchical, functional, divisional forms of organization are giving way to more flexible, dynamic, loose forms (Ruekert, Walker, and Roering 1985).

Author's note: This paper has benefited immeasurably from suggestions and comments on earlier drafts by Gert Assmus, Stephan Haeckel, David Montgomery, Scott Neslin, and David Ulrich. The remaining errors, inconsistencies, and ambiguities are clearly my responsibility.

Consider the various forms of re-engineering, downsizing, de-layering, and networking that have gained such popularity. In the words of Peter Drucker, "Information is replacing authority," as the basic control mechanism in organizations and "Corporations built to last like pyramids are now more like tents." (Harris 1993, p. 116). Among the more profound implications of this change are: (1) a blurring of the distinction between strategy and organization (Haeckel and Nolan 1993; Haeckel 1995b; Slywotzky 1996); (2) a redefinition of marketing as a set of interlinked value-delivery processes instead of a management function with distinct responsibilities (Day 1995; Webster 1994); and (3) a fundamental questioning of the idea that organization structure is a vehicle for implementing strategy.

Since the pioneering work of Alfred D. Chandler (1962), it has been a basic tenet of management theory that structure follows strategy (a nice parallel to Louis Sullivan's architectural insight that form follows function). Strategy and structure, as well as culture, have long been regarded as fundamentally distinct management concepts. This traditional distinction is becoming obsolete with a new understanding of the critical importance of creating dynamic, responsive systems for delivering superior value to customers whose definition of value keeps changing (Slywotzky 1996; Webster 1994). In fact, the inherently static concept of structure is strangely at odds with this fundamental strategic fact of life—as new information is obtained and analyzed and new buying needs, preferences, priorities, and habits emerge, the customer's definition of value is by its nature dynamic.

If marketing is to survive into the 21st century as an identifiable (although not necessarily *distinct*) management function, it must address some shortcomings in its ability to contribute to the strategy and business design dialogue within the firm by integrating its cultural, strategic, and tactical dimensions. The good news for marketers is that, in doing so, marketing may, at last, fulfill its vision of a truly customer-oriented firm. As the distinction between strategy and organization blurs, and network forms of organization emerge, marketing may well assume a leadership role in the organization as customer advocate and expert.

At this point, the reader might find a roadmap helpful. The purpose of this chapter, then, is to define some of the issues inherent in traditional approaches to marketing organization. I will suggest that marketing management's historical origin as an adjunct to the sales function has resulted in persistent confusion between marketing as strategy and marketing as tactics. The marketing concept, emphasizing a culture of customer orientation, was developed in an attempt to correct the short-term, opportunistic orientation of the typical sales and marketing organization. Likewise, strategic planning as a discipline was developed, at least in part, as an antidote to the internal, tactical emphasis on sales volume. Paradoxically, however, the strategic role of marketing has suffered—both in practice and in the development of a sound body of theoretical and empirical knowledge—under the hegemony of strategic planning. I will identify several environmental and organizational forces that are shaping our understanding of marketing as a value-delivery process and consider a view of marketing that focuses on organizational processes and capabilities. I will conclude with some conjectures about the characteristics of marketing within successful organizations in the next decade.

Traditional Forms of Marketing Organization

Since the 1920s, when marketing was first defined as a separate business function, discussions about how marketing should be organized have implicitly assumed that the parent or host organization was the traditional corporate form: multidivisional, multiproduct, hierarchical, and bureaucratic. Right through the 1960s and into the 1970s, this hierarchical corporate form—as first found in the Roman Catholic Church and the military and then applied to business organizations—was heralded as one of the most significant innovations of the industrial age (Blau 1956). The design of these organizations was guided by generally accepted organizational principles such as:

> ➤ *Unity of command*—every person should have a reporting relationship to only one supervisor

➤ *Span of control*—any manager should be responsible for a small number of subordinates, often said to be five to seven

➤ *Authority commensurate with responsibility*—each member of the organization should control the people and other resources necessary to perform assigned duties

➤ *Clarity*—the authority and responsibility of each position should be clearly defined in a written job description

➤ *Redundancy avoidance*—overlapping, duplicative, and conflicting job responsibilities should be eliminated

Organizations were thought of as command structures defining superior/subordinate relationships. Organization design was guided by the twin criteria of effectiveness and efficiency, which were often in conflict and required compromise. The ultimate goal was to be sure all marketing functions were performed with the highest probability of achieving the firm's objectives at the lowest possible cost.

In terms of organizational design, marketing managers could choose among four basic forms: functional, product, market or end-use oriented, geographic, or some combination of these (Corey and Star 1971; Weitz and Anderson 1981). Other conceptual issues were whether marketing should be at the corporate or divisional level, whether it was a line or staff function, and whether the salesforce was part of the marketing function.

The *functional* form of organization was common. Standard marketing organizations included a basic set of functions: market research, sales, and advertising and sales promotion. These marketing functions were originally added to traditional sales organizations as a way of improving sales effectiveness and coordinating sales with production, finance, and other basic activities. Market research and analysis led to improved sales forecasting and production planning as well as more objective methods of establishing sales quotas and other performance measures. Advertising, sales promotion, and other communications activities were handled by specialists in the graphic arts and the preparation of printed materials. Gradually, other functions, including product planning and management, pricing, and distribution, were also incorporated into many marketing departments. More specialized functions such as marketing planning and public relations and publicity were also sometimes included.

With Procter & Gamble as the pioneer in the late 1920s, many consumer packaged goods companies developed a brand manager or *product* manager form of organization. Its purpose was to facilitate the marketing of potentially competing products aimed at distinct market segments. A variety of product management forms evolved but in each a single manager was responsible for most of the marketing functions associated with a given product or group of products, *with the notable exception of the sales function, which remained independent.* Thus, product managers typically had to compete among themselves for a portion of the time of the salesforce.

In other companies, usually those selling to industrial customers, a *market* or *end-user* form of organization was found, with separate marketing organizations for particular industries or other groupings of customers. Yet another standard form of marketing organization was regional or *geographic* in nature, with organizations for particular areas such as the eastern, midwestern, and western United States. Each region might have its own distinct marketing functions or those might be found in a centralized, functional marketing organization at the national headquarters level. Clearly, in the regional organization form, the logic of the salesforce organization dominated the organization of the marketing function, consistent with an implicit assumption that marketing was in essence a sales support, rather than strategic, function.

Some marketing historians would argue that there was an evolutionary trend from functional to product to market organizations, although there are many exceptions to this pattern.

A more complicated form, a *matrix* marketing organization, violated the principle of unity of command by establishing two reporting relationships, typically to a geographic manager and a product or market manager. This was seen, for example, in the position of a field marketing manager in a chemical company who might report to both the Midwest region sales manager, say, in the Cleveland sales office and a Polyolefins product manager at corporate headquarters in New York.

Implicit in the design of these traditional marketing organizations were five assumptions:

1. Subject to only slight variation, there is a small and definable set of marketing organization structures, namely, the four outlined above.

2. The organization structure should match the firm's basic marketing strategy.

3. Both strategy and structure should have some long-term permanence.

4. There is a definable set of business functions that are the legitimate domain of professional marketing managers.

5. The fundamental purpose of the marketing department is to generate and stimulate demand for the firm's production.

Each of these assumptions requires careful re-examination in creating the marketing organization of the future.

The Conflict within Marketing as Culture, Strategy, and Tactics

The marketing concept, as articulated in the 1950s, was a response to the perception that the marketing function tended to concentrate primarily on the objective of generating demand for production output. Thus, the typical marketing department was short term and tactical in its orientation. The marketing concept, on the other hand, called for a long-term, strategic orientation focused on satisfying customer needs with an integrated strategy encompassing product, pricing, promotion, and distribution. It also described an organizational culture, a set of shared values and beliefs, that put the customer's interests first. Profit was seen as the reward for creating customer satisfaction. Although the marketing concept was widely accepted as a management philosophy in many companies, sales and product orientation continued to drive out customer and profit orientation (Hise 1965; Kaldor 1971; McNamara 1972; Webster 1981, 1988). The reasons for this have never been well understood. However, part of the explanation certainly lies with the short-term, quarterly earnings orientation that dominates performance measurement systems in most publicly owned corporations (Hayes and Abernathy 1980; Webster 1981). When top management spends so much time under the klieg lights of financial analysts and powerful institutional investors, they inevitably focus on shareholders rather than on customers. Measurement criteria for customer orientation and its (long-term) impact on business performance are much harder to define than (short-term) sales, profitability, and return-on-investment results. In addition, in many companies, marketing managers come into their positions from the sales organization and have not been trained to think strategically and in the long term. At a more abstract level, the marketing concept's dictum that marketing is everyone's responsibility (in the sense that it is "the whole business seen from the customer's point of view") has tended to mean, in practice, that marketing is nobody's responsibility.

Furthermore, the relationship between the sales and marketing functions has persisted as one of the major sources of organizational conflict. As noted earlier, marketing typically originated within the sales department to provide support in areas such as advertising, sales promotion, and market research. Eventually, it evolved into a separate function and became independent of the sales department. This separation proved to be unstable, however, as each duplicated some of the functions of the other, especially in such areas as product management and industry/market specialization. The result was confusion over organizational responsibility for various products and market segments, producing frustration on the part of key customers as well as within the organization itself. Under the pressures of re-engineering and other forms of cost reduction, marketing organizations have been downsized to reduce redundancy; however, the appropriate relationship between the sales and the marketing functions is still an unresolved issue.

Marketing's Failure as Strategy

Since marketing encompasses culture, strategy, and tactics, the marketing department faces a complex, and perhaps unreasonable, challenge. It must simultaneously:

> ➤ Advocate the customer's point of view throughout the organization, keeping all decision makers informed about the customer's needs and wants, building a culture of customer orientation under the leadership of top management

> ➤ Analyze markets and define market segments, select customer groupings to be the target for the firm's marketing efforts, match customer needs with company capabilities, and develop a value proposition and competitive positioning to guide the organization

> ➤ Develop detailed marketing plans in the areas of product management, pricing, promotion, and channels of distribution that will implement the overall business strategy and achieve the desired levels of sales, market share, and profitability

It is generally agreed that marketing departments have been most effective in the last area (tactics), somewhat effective in the first area (culture), and least effective in the area of strategy (Day 1992; Ruekert et al. 1985; Varadarajan 1992). (However, some would argue that marketing *has* had significant strategic impact in many firms, especially in the market segmentation and targeting area.) Let us look more closely at the reasons for marketing's apparent failure in the strategy area.

H. Igor Ansoff (1965) describes in detail the process by which formal strategic planning came into being as a distinct management function. Briefly, we can note that strategic planning evolved out of long-range (production) planning in response to some perceived shortcomings in the marketing concept (Webster 1992, 1994). The marketing concept, while it championed a customer orientation, tended to ignore the issue of defining the firm's essential strengths or "core competencies" as the basis for its strategic selection of markets and products (Kaldor 1971). In fact, Ansoff, the father of strategic planning, argued that marketing "strategy" was not a strategic function at all, but a series of operating decisions (Ansoff 1965, pp. 5, 93). This narrowed the scope of marketing and confined it to the tactical areas of management decision.

In several companies, most prominently General Electric, a formal strategic planning function was developed in the late 1960s to address these shortcomings and to strengthen the implementation of the marketing concept. However, as strategic planning gained popularity in the 1960s and 1970s and formal strategic planning departments ascended to preeminent positions in the corporate hierarchy, strategic planning and marketing became distinct management functions and were organized in separate departments. In many companies, some of the best marketing strategists moved out of marketing and into the new strategic planning departments (Webster 1981). Further, strategic thinking became increasingly industry centered, not customer centered (Slywotzky 1996, p. 132). The strategic focus was on the firm's strengths and weaknesses relative to its competitors' in such areas as production capacity, economies of scale, market share, and turnover of assets. Markets were defined as collections of competitors, not customers.

For the better part of two decades, the best business opportunities were thought to be in the fastest-growing areas where the firm could achieve a dominant share of market. Discussions of business strategy were often organized around the relative merits of the (false) dichotomy of either low-cost or high-quality (market-niching) strategies.

In other words, marketing and customer orientation had largely disappeared from the strategy dialogue in many companies by the early 1970s. Strategic issues tended to be addressed in the context of internal, operations-, industry-, and financially oriented thinking. Marketing tactics were dominated by competitor focus (evidenced by the preoccupation with market share) and internal needs (e.g., for so much production in a given quarter), rather than by the customer focus of the marketing concept. The lack of clear, customer-driven marketing strategy led to a fundamental disconnect between marketing culture and marketing tactics. Lip service paid to customer orientation as a management philosophy was devoid of strategic content. Strategy emphasized achieving low cost and meeting production and financial budget requirements, rather than delivering superior value to customers.

Ruekert et al. (1985) argue that the short-term financial orientation engendered by strategic planning resulted in organization structures that were centralized, formalized, and bureaucratic in order to achieve the degree of control necessary to meet those short-term performance criteria. Thus, a short-term focus on efficiency exacted a high price in long-term organizational effectiveness and adaptiveness.

Marketing had often failed to perform its basic strategic management functions:

1. Market segmentation and targeting—analyzing markets to define differences in customer needs, preferences, and priorities and selecting those segments where the firm is best able to achieve unique competitive advantage

2. Developing the value proposition—matching the firm's resources, capabilities, and "distinctive competence" with a carefully defined set of customer needs; positioning the firm in the value chain

3. Supply chain design and management—developing and managing relationships with various resource providers, including resellers and product/service vendors, in order to provide a total product/service offering that is consistent with the firm's value proposition

The so-called "strategic" role of marketing was often limited to the short-term tactical areas of demand stimulation including price promotions, advertising, selling, and some aspects of distribution management. Even in the area of marketing communications, time and money were allocated primarily to short-term sales inducements such as price reductions rather than long-term investments in building brand equity (Blattberg and Neslin 1989). In many companies, marketing is still essentially a sales support function, subordinate to a strong sales department and national account management program. Important strategic questions in the design and management of procurement and distribution strategy were commonly made the responsibility of operations management, which inevitably led to a focus on short-term cost and efficiency. For the past two or three decades, marketing has effectively ceded its strategic responsibilities to other organizational specialists who have not, until recently, been guided by the voice of the customer.

We don't have to look far to see the consequences, often disastrous, of the loss of strategic focus on the customer. In industries as diverse as airlines, computers, electronics, financial services, housewares, retailing, steel, and tires, one-time industry leaders have been driven into decline, bankruptcy, and oblivion by new market entrants and smaller competitors, often from outside traditionally defined industry (and country) boundaries, with superior value propositions and value delivery systems for customers (Slywotzky 1996). In most of these diminished firms, marketing can be anything but proud of its performance.

Forces Reshaping the Marketing Function

By the early 1980s, however, the strategic planning fad had sub-
sided (Kiechel 1982) as many companies became frightened by the
size and expense (in time and dollar expenditures) of their strategic
planning bureaucracies and by the realization that market share often
did not translate into profitability, especially when low price was the
vehicle by which share was achieved. There was a basic mismatch
between the formal, bureaucratic discipline of strategic planning and
increasingly changeable markets. Total quality management emerged
as a more important value and discipline in a market environment
characterized by global competitors and increasingly sophisticated and
demanding customers. Even those who had most strongly advocated
market share as the key to profitability came around to the point of
view that *quality* was the fundamental driver of business performance
and profitability (Buzzell and Gale 1987). Paradoxically, the total
quality movement (with its roots in operations management, not marketing) and its various tributaries, including re-engineering, have had
a significant influence in reintroducing customer orientation into
many organizations. One of the most interesting developments of the
1990s has been the renewed widespread interest in customer focus as
a management concept (Blattberg 1995; Webster 1988, 1992;
Whiteley 1991). The technology- and product-driven strategies of
previous decades are no longer an adequate source of unique or sus-
tainable competitive advantage because they are so easily and quickly
copied (Slywotzky 1996).

Increasingly sophisticated customers are a major force for improved
marketing performance. Much attention has been paid to the concept
of organizational learning. Equally important is the concept of customer learning. As competitors battle for the customer's patronage,
they educate the customer. Customers become better informed, more
knowledgeable, and more sophisticated in their choice processes. They
become less dependent on a given supplier for product knowledge and
service and better able to understand market options as well as their
own use situation. They gain confidence in their ability to make

informed choices and they gain power in their negotiations with various sellers. This is not to imply that buyer-seller relationships become more adversarial. They may, in fact, become more focused on building mutually satisfying buyer-seller partnerships with an equitable sharing of value between the parties.

Thus, the focus of marketing has shifted from *single transactions* to *long-term customer relationships*. Such relationships are anything but static; marketing in the 21st century must deal with customers whose definition of value changes at an increasing rate, thanks to the influences of global competition and information technology. This is an essential point for the future of marketing organization: a dynamic concept of customer value requires dynamic marketing strategy and organization. Neither strategy nor organization can be thought of as a "correct" or semi-permanent positioning of the firm in the competitive arena; both must be reconceptualized as a process for responding to the needs and priorities of customers whose definition of value is constantly evolving (Webster 1994). Haeckel (1995a, b) sees this as a movement from "make and sell" to "sense and respond," from a mindset of products and transactions to one of capabilities and relationships, from organizational priorities of efficiency and predictability to flexibility and responsiveness. Instead of thinking of strategy as planning, implemented through a hierarchical command and control structure, strategy is reconceptualized as adaptive structure design implemented through dynamic networks of organizational actors. The strategic process is the continuous redesign and improvement of the business itself as a set of activities for delivering value to customers (Slywotzky 1996).

In this regard, one of the most significant forces reshaping marketing is *information technology* (Blattberg 1995) which provides the linkages necessary for customers and marketers to develop and maintain mutually beneficial relationships in a changing environment. Using a continuous flow of current information, companies can design product offerings tailored to the needs of individual customers and market segments. At the extreme, we have "markets of one" and "mass customization" (Pine 1993).

The concept of *network organization* also depends heavily on information technology, which enables the seamless integration of multiple service providers in the value chain to produce the final product offering to the customer. Suppliers of products, transportation, credit, technical support, and a variety of other dimensions of a total product offering may be tied together at a single point by telecommunications and database capabilities that are coordinated by a marketer who in fact outsources all of these other functions. (Examples include Calyx and Corolla providing fresh flowers and Monsanto's Protiva selling recombinant bovine growth hormone direct to farmers.) The company is defined by its customers, not its products. The product is no longer a "given" which the organization tries to "market" (i.e., sell) through its marketing activities. The product is a variable, tailored to the changing needs of carefully selected customers. As the customer changes, so must the product, and the organization that provides that product must have built-in flexibility and adaptiveness.

To summarize, the forces reshaping marketing organizations include customer focus, information technology, globalization, customer relationships, concepts of organizational learning and adaptation (including team-centered management), networks and flexible organization forms, and a redefinition of marketing as a value-delivery process.

Marketing as a Value-Delivery Process

To say that a business is defined by its customers is still a radical idea for most companies, even though this was the premise of the marketing concept when it was developed more than 40 years ago. However, the concept of customer value provides a mechanism for integrating the cultural, strategic, and tactical dimensions of marketing.

Marketing can be thought of as the design and management of all of the business processes necessary to define, develop, and deliver value to customers. These processes consist of sets of interdependent activities, some of which are traditional marketing activities and others of which have traditionally been organized under the functional rubric of production or operations. In other words, a marketing process is any business process that gathers information from customers, is guided by information about customers, or produces outputs that are used and evaluated by customers. A list of marketing processes might include the following:

Value-defining processes:

> Market research—studies of customer needs, preferences, buying behavior, product use, etc.

> Analysis of core competencies

> Strategic positioning of the firm in the value chain

> Economic analysis of customer use systems

Value-developing processes:

> New product development

> Design of distribution channels

> Development of procurement strategy

> Vendor selection

> Strategic partnering with service providers (e.g., credit, database management, product service and disposal)

> Developing pricing strategy

> Developing the value proposition

Value-delivering processes:

> Managing distribution and logistics

> Deployment of the field salesforce

> Order-entry, credit, and post-sales service

> Advertising and sales promotion

➤ Applications engineering

➤ Product upgrades and recalls

➤ Customer training

Many of the business processes that are involved in defining, developing, and delivering value to customers have been the responsibility of the operations management side of the business, the functions of engineering, manufacturing, purchasing, and logistics. Each of those has traditionally been managed with a primary focus on efficiency and cost control. However, as sophisticated customers began to demand better quality in all aspects of the value-delivery process including distribution, product design, inventory management, and many other functions, operations management became increasingly customer driven. British Airways, for example, has reorganized its operations to put them under the control of marketing, which now encompasses 80 percent of its employees, based on the realization that the two most important service dimensions, safety and reliability, were the responsibility of operations managers. It made sense to be sure that these processes were customer driven.

It should be an embarrassment to marketers that the quality movement came out of operations, rather than marketing. Operations management in hundreds of manufacturing firms, often under pressure from key customers such as Motorola or Ford with state-of-the-art total quality management systems, came to understand that quality must be defined as meeting customer needs, not as simply minimizing errors in production and reducing costs. Marketing managers were asleep at the switch, having lost the focus on customer needs in pursuit of short-term sales volume and market share. In simple terms, it was the operations emphasis on cost and the marketing/sales emphasis on sales volume that caused many firms to lose ground to competitors, often from Asia, who had a better focus on the customer and the customer's changing definition of value. Automobiles, consumer electronics, photography, stock brokerage, and chemicals are examples of industries where this pattern has been observed.

Characteristics of Future Marketing Organizations

The new marketing paradigm, with its focus on processes for defining, developing, and delivering customer value, has a number of profound implications for marketing organization. First, it suggests that marketing organizations must be highly flexible and dynamic. Second, defining organizations around marketing functions or products or markets is likely to lead to inflexibility and lack of responsiveness to changing market conditions, including customer priorities and competitive moves. Third, the new marketing paradigm operates on the assumption that no firm, no matter how large, can command all of the resources and competencies necessary to produce the highest possible value for customers within the boundaries of its own organization. Rather, the company must work with strategic partners in many areas, including technology development, product design, manufacturing, transportation, selling, service, and so on, in order to provide the maximum value to its customers. A key role for marketing managers in this new type of organization is to design and manage this multitude of strategic partnerships. Because the process must start and end with the customer, not the product, marketing has the key role to play in the management of these teams of individual functional experts.

Because customers are constantly changing, the organization must continuously innovate, experiment, and redesign its value-delivery processes. This calls for a mindset fundamentally different from the old strategy-structure paradigm.

How, then, does one predict the shape of future marketing organizations? It will not be possible to visualize them with the tools of the standard organization chart. In fact, it is questionable whether we will be able to identify a traditional marketing function as a separate organizational activity per se.

A traditional, though mistaken, approach would be to try to predict the future and then to develop a strategy and an organization to "fit" that strategy. Organizations must instead develop the capability to monitor the changing environment of customers and competitors and adapt quickly to any (reasonable) future state of the world and the strategy appropriate to it. In fact, organization for the future is not structure per se; it is *capability* for responding to the changing environment. Marketing will be responsible for managing not only relationships with customers but also relationships with other providers of customer value, keeping these strategic partners focused on the firm's customers and their changing definition of value. The critical strategic issue will be which of the partners "owns the customer" because that will define the control point in the value chain.

Marketing Capabilities

In place of the simplistic strategy → structure paradigm of bureaucracy, the design of marketing organizations for the future will be guided by a more complex paradigm of processes → capabilities → form.[1] First, the organization analyst must define the marketing activities and processes within the organization. Second, the analyst must identify the specific analytical and management capabilities required to design and manage those processes (Day 1994). Third, the analyst must put together flexible, dynamic, responsive organization forms to integrate those capabilities and to implement the value-delivery processes. Of fundamental importance, the design must be guided by the best possible information about the customer's definition of value. Information about customers and processes for disseminating, analyzing, and using that information are the key linking mechanisms for the organization (Barabba 1995). Thus "the voice of the customer" provides the critical connection between an organizational culture of values and beliefs that put the customer first and an effective strategic response in terms of products and services aimed at carefully defined target markets.

---

[1] *I have borrowed this idea from Professor David Ulrich of the University of Michigan, based on a private conversation. In his words, the process must move from a "two-step dance" to a "three-step dance."*

Organizations developing the new paradigm must break new ground in defining marketing processes and marketing capabilities as well as in structuring new forms of marketing organization. Authors of other chapters in this volume, especially Day, also deal specifically with these issues of defining marketing skills, competencies, and capabilities. Here I will simply try to sketch some preliminary thoughts about an integrated design for future marketing organizations.

Marketing processes—the intellectual and organizational domain of the marketing function—were defined earlier as those which either gather information from and about customers, use information about customers to design and manage that process, or produce outputs that are used and evaluated by customers. It would seem obvious that any such process should be customer focused. However, we know from experience that this is not always the case. Billing processes, for example, produce outputs that are used and evaluated by customers but are seldom designed and managed from a customer perspective.

Clearly, marketing processes will overlap with processes in other functional domains; my argument is that all such processes should be managed from a customer-value perspective. Inventory management, for example, fits the definition of a marketing process but it is also part of one or more manufacturing processes. Thus, managers from both marketing and manufacturing (and probably finance as well), must be involved in the design and management of inventory management systems. In fact, just-in-time inventory systems provide an excellent example of a value-delivery process guided by the customer's needs rather than traditional internally focused cost control (Karmarkar 1996).

The question arises, Which of the traditional management "functions" should provide the guidance mechanism, the criteria by which performance is evaluated, especially when choices must be made about the allocation of scarce resources? The logic of customer orientation (and total quality management) asserts that the customer's interest should dominate. In this case, a manufacturing specialist with the relevant skills in production forecasting, planning, scheduling, and capacity utilization may be the best leader for the inventory management process—only if, however, he or she is provided with the best possible information about customer needs, wants, buying patterns, and priorities. The manufacturing manager must be customer oriented and the inventory management process must be customer driven.

The logic of value delivery leads inevitably to a concept of team management. Management authors in many fields agree that teams will be increasingly common organizational mechanisms in the flexible, dynamic, networked organizations of the future. These teams will consist of both functional specialists and general managers whose skills are those of coordination and integration (George, Freeling, and Court 1994; Harris 1993). As a general rule, the role of the marketing person is to keep the team focused on the customer and the changing definition of value, to function as a teacher to the team conveying useful knowledge about customers and competitive activities. Obviously, marketing specialists in particular areas such as pricing or product development or advertising will have specific knowledge and skills to contribute to the team's work.

A. T. Kearney, management consultants, identify four key marketing processes, based on their research at 26 major U.S. companies (Bluestein 1994). These processes are:

1. Establishing a competitive position

2. Defining target markets and designing products/services to serve these markets

3. Delivering products/services to target markets

4. Creating and managing demand

The first three of these processes could be described as strategic whereas the fourth is more tactical. The Kearney research concluded that managers in best-practice companies were focused on marketing as a process rather than a function and had made marketing the facilitator in multifunctional teams, keeping them focused on the customer. The essential capabilities for marketing managers in this organizational context are teamwork, innovation, and integration.

Thomas M. Beddow (1995) has described how 3M Company defines marketing "competencies," which encompasses both processes and capabilities, as follows:

Core Marketing Competencies:

➤ Planning—defining the business and its customers

➤ Product development—strategy for business unit growth

➤ Value pricing—understanding the utility the customer places on the company's products and services

➤ Channel management—developing and managing the institutions through which the company goes to market

➤ Customer analysis—analyzing individuals, organizations, and institutions in terms of needs, desires, and ability to buy

➤ Research—gathering and interpreting market information for marketing decision making

➤ Brand management—developing and managing strong global brands and corporate assets

Advanced Marketing Competencies:

➤ International—marketing products and services across national borders

➤ Financial analysis—identifying profitable strategies that increase the lifetime value of the customer

➤ Strategic planning—developing strategic fit between organizational goals and capabilities and changing market opportunities

➤ Quality Function Deployment—translating customer inputs into design requirements

➤ Process management—Interrelating critical organizational functions in product development, manufacturing, selling, and distribution

➤ Value added—continually improving customer value

➤ Customer-focused selling—demonstrating a consistent ability to meet and exceed customer expectations

Complementary Marketing Competencies:

➤ Teamwork—ability to function as a member of a cross-functional team

➤ Interpersonal skills—ability to listen and understand the needs of others, to manage conflict, and to convey information

➤ Marketing communications—exchange of product information between buyers and sellers

➤ Computer literacy—ability to use data retrieval systems, develop databases, apply computer-based models, etc.

Beddow's concept of competencies draws together individual skills and knowledge, on the one hand, and organizational processes for information development, exchange, and utilization on the other. Others make a stronger distinction between individual-level skills and organizational capabilities.

It can be argued that the old functional view of marketing (market research, product development, pricing, advertising, selling, etc.) placed a heavy emphasis on individual skills in information gathering, data analysis, and (external) persuasion. Marketers were either "researchers" or "hucksters." In the new paradigm, the critical marketing skills include negotiation, conflict resolution, relationship management, internal communication and persuasion, managing interfaces, team building, teaching, information interpretation, and strategic reasoning.

Stages in the Evolution of Marketing Organizations

We are now in a position to review the development of marketing organization in the past, summarize the forces shaping it in the present, and try to project its evolution into the future. Following the historical development of marketing organizations and the analysis and arguments put forth in this paper, it is possible to think of the development of marketing organizations as occurring in a sequence of phases.

The first phase equates marketing with sales. The emphasis is on generating demand for the company's productive resources, a short-term tactical focus. In the second phase, marketing specialists in areas like marketing research and sales promotion are brought into the sales organization and given budgets that implement a formal planning and control process in pursuit of short-term financial objectives. A bureaucratic, hierarchical organizational form is put in place to monitor and control performance against budget. This phase may involve creating product or market management organizations, or a matrix of the two forms.

In phase three, marketing becomes a distinct function, separate from sales, and pursues excellence in all phases of integrated marketing strategy, including market segmentation and targeting, product development and positioning, advertising and promotion, pricing, and distribution. Phase three companies experience ongoing conflict between marketing and sales and weak integration of marketing with other business functions. These "functional silos" or "chimneys" of phase three organizations slow response to the changing market environment.

In the fourth phase, which will characterize successful companies in the future, marketing competence is integrated with other business functions in team-centered organizational processes that are focused on the customer. Until recently, phase three companies were likely to be held up as models of marketing excellence. In the future, phase four companies will lead the way to improved marketing practice.

In phase four companies, marketing will play different roles at different points in the organization. Functional silos will break down and the organization will increasingly consist of linkages with other partners in the value chain; however, there will still be a skeletal structure of the corporation with its headquarters, strategic business units, and functional specialists. Marketing competence will be necessary at all levels, but the activities and responsibilities of the people responsible for marketing will be very different (Webster 1992).

At the top management levels of the organization, marketing responsibility includes customer advocacy and development of a culture of customer orientation. This responsibility rests on the shoulders of the chief executive officer, the chief operating officer, and their supporting staff. Marketing analysis at this level includes understanding the firm's distinctive competencies and capabilities, and the dynamics of customer needs and competitive product offerings (as the interaction of these creates opportunities for the company). At the level of corporate strategy, marketing expertise can provide valuable information and strategic thinking to answer the question, "What businesses do we want to be in?" Marketing should guide the strategic process of matching customer needs and the company's core competencies.

At the level of the strategic business unit (product/market combinations), marketing managers should have responsibility for market segmentation and targeting analysis, for defining the firm's value proposition to its chosen customers, and for defining and managing the firm's positioning in the value chain. The combination of the value proposition and the marketing mechanisms for taking the product offering to market (sales, distribution, and customer service activities) define the basic business design that is the firm's answer to the business strategy question: "How do we want to compete in the businesses we have chosen to be in?" At the business-unit level, marketing has general responsibility for keeping all of the decision makers focused on the customers and their changing definitions of value.

Finally, at the functional, tactical level of implementing the business strategy, marketing specialists are responsible for developing specific product and branding strategies, marketing communications, and distribution strategies consistent with the value proposition to deliver superior value to customers. Marketing is specifically responsible for measuring, managing, and meeting customer expectations, and for managing strategic relationships with customers. The marketing specialists must develop programs for spending resources in ways that not only maximize customer satisfaction but that earn superior returns on the firm's investment.

Translating customer value into shareholder value is the final test for management, but it is the customer value that drives the profit result. Recent research on customer orientation, organization culture, and innovation supports the argument that all three have a significant influence on the performance of the firm, as measured by return on investment and rate of growth. The best-performing firms are highly innovative, have an external focus on the marketplace (rather than an internal focus on the organization itself), and use flexible rather than bureaucratic forms of organization (Deshpandé, Farley, and Webster 1993).

Summary and Conclusions

I have looked at the shift of marketing thinking from a functional/structural focus to an activities/processes/capabilities focus. I have tried to sort out and then reintegrate the cultural, strategic, and tactical dimensions of marketing. A central theme was marketing's abdication of its strategic responsibilities in the past and the current need to develop and reassert a customer-focused strategic thrust if the firm is to survive in the competitive marketplace. In particular, I have argued that marketing must play a strategic role in designing and guiding many management processes that have been the responsibility of strategic planning and operations management. These include positioning the firm in the value chain, market sensing, customer linking, and supply chain management.

Strategic planning must be customer focused and market driven. Marketing management should be responsible for designing and guiding the multiple processes of value delivery within the firm. To be effective, marketing managers will need new skills in information collection and analysis, team management, teaching, negotiation, and relationship management. These are required not only for managing the interfaces with other functional managers within the company but also for developing and managing relationships with strategic partners from outside the firm, including vendors, resellers, and other service providers.

Organizations that survive into the next century will be those that know their basic competencies and allow themselves to be defined by their customers in terms of capabilities and processes required to deliver superior value. As those customers change their definition of value and their priorities, so must the organization's capabilities grow and their processes change. While it is foolhardy to try to predict what the marketing organization of the future will "look like" in the traditional sense, I would put forward these concluding conjectures:

1. The successful organization of the future will be customer focused, not product or technology focused, supported by a market-information competence that links the voice of the customer to all of the firm's value-delivery processes.

2. Customer relationships, more than products, will be seen as the critical strategic assets of the business and this will be reflected in organizational arrangements with key customers and reseller partners. Successful marketing organizations will be structured around major customers and markets, not products, and will integrate sales, product strategy, distribution, and marketing communications competencies and activities.

3. Business strategies and organizational arrangements will be linked by customer-driven value-delivery processes that are continuously modified and improved in response to changing customer needs and priorities. Strategies, capabilities, processes, and organization will all evolve in

response to the changing market environment. The more dynamic the environment, the more flexible the successful organization must be.

4. The most serious competitive threats for many firms will come from competitors who fundamentally redesign their systems for going to market, not their products per se. The organization itself, and its capabilities, will be the major competitive weapon. Customers will increasingly tend to buy the firm's value-delivery system, not its products.

5. Successful marketing organizations will have the skills necessary to manage multiple *strategic* marketing processes, many of which have not, until recently, been regarded as within the domain of marketing, including:

> ➤ Understanding the firm's core competencies

> ➤ Positioning the firm in the value chain

> ➤ Defining the need for strategic partners

> ➤ Market segmentation and targeting

> ➤ Developing value propositions for target markets

> ➤ Supply chain management—configuring the firm's value-delivery capabilities and those of strategic partners with capabilities at other points in the value chain, including resellers and vendors

> ➤ Customer linking—managing long-term, strategic relationships with end-users and resellers

> ➤ Market sensing—data collection, plus analysis, interpretation, and dissemination, for tracking customers' changing definition of value and competitive value propositions and delivery system performance

> ➤ Product offering development—innovation in processes of value delivery

There was a time when I, and others, argued that "marketing is too important to be left to the marketing people." In retrospect, that was misleading. If marketing is everybody's responsibility, it ends up being nobody's responsibility and the marketing skills of the organization atrophy. Marketing specialists are needed, and must take responsibility, for skills in the areas outlined above and for keeping the entire organization focused on the customer. What I should have said was, "Customer orientation is too important to be left to the marketing people." Delivering superior value to customers is the ultimate responsibility of every person in the organization. If not, the value of the firm is diminished. ■

➤ 4

Aligning the Organization to the Market

George S. Day

Had we been contemplating the future of marketing a decade ago, organizational issues would have been at the periphery. Who would have challenged the prevailing functional design, with a hierarchical command and control framework,[1] or the product management system? Acceptance didn't mean satisfaction, for there were ongoing adjustments to the balance of centralization/decentralization and attempts to clarify the ambiguity of matrix structures, as well as a growing realization of the importance of culture and some concern about the rigidities of functionally based structures. However, the overall stability that seemed to prevail was deceptive.

As we approach the millennium, organizational issues are rising to the top of the agenda on the future of marketing. The leading indicators of this shift in priority were the criticisms of marketing in industries that were thought to be highly proficient marketers. Marketing was variously described as "in the midst of a mid-life crisis, . . . failing to live up to its pretensions, . . . rarely leading the drive to enhance performance;" marketing departments, it was said, were "struggling with diminished stature and thinning ranks."[2] Ironically, as

---

1. *Fred Webster describes these traditionally accepted organizations more fully in his chapter in this volume, "The Future Role of Marketing in the Organization."*

2. *These quotes were selected from:* Reinventing Brand Management, *Boston: Boston Consulting Group, April 1994;* Marketing at the Crossroads, *London: Coopers & Lybrand, 1994; and* Marketing Metamorphosis, *New York: McKinsey & Co., 1994.*

the functional role of marketing was eroding, the need for an organi-
zation-wide orientation to the market was increasingly accepted and
endorsed. This was driven by top management and by operations,
both following the edict of total quality management (TQM) to focus
all employees on continuous improvement in the eyes of the customer
(Schonberger 1992).

In retrospect, the angst about the role of the marketing function
was an inevitable by-product of disruptive changes in most markets
and the emergence of new organizational models that challenged traditional approaches. These forces have been building during the past
decade, but have only recently coalesced to force a complete rethinking of the future of marketing in its various roles as management
function, strategic guidance mechanism, specialized knowledge
resource, and organizational orientation offering an integrating logic.

This rethinking process is guided by the belief that success comes
by aligning the strategy and capabilities of the organization with the
market, thereby delivering superior customer value. The challenge is to
deal with the disruptive effects of market fragmentation, rising customer expectations, intensifying competition, and channel diversity
while innovating at an accelerating pace. An organization that stays in
alignment with its markets must change its structures, roles, and activities when customer requirements and standards change. It should be
the customer who drives the organization—not the other way around.

The *reality* of an organization will inevitably fall short of the *ideal*
of a continuously adaptive alignment of strategies, activities, and distinctive capabilities with shifting market requirements. Whatever
structure is chosen will be a compromise that balances numerous con-
tending forces (Cespedes 1995):

> ➤ Make it new and innovative vs. Be predictable and con-
>   sistent

> ➤ Maintain flexibility with small units vs. Achieve
>   economies of scale

> ➤ Develop deep functional expertise through speculation vs. Subordinate functions to teams managing linked processes

> ➤ Facilitate coordination and information sharing vs. Eliminate overhead and nonproductive activities

Once the organization is in place and seems to be functioning properly, a combination of inertia and a tendency to build on the knowledge and skills that are already in place constrains future choices to a narrower path. This makes further changes more difficult (Liebowitz and Margolis 1995).

Nevertheless, firms *are* learning to narrow and even eliminate the gap between reality and the ideal of continuously adaptive alignment. They are doing so by adopting recent innovations in hybrid or hypertext organizational designs and exploiting the power of dispersed information networks. In this chapter I will show how these two developments are shaping the future of organizations and thus changing the role of marketing.

As organizations strive to become fast moving and customer responsive, will marketing be the dominant integrating force, as marketers like to assert, or a support activity subordinated to a strong leader or the business development function? Where will deep market knowledge and market expertise be located, and how will it be provided to the rest of the organization? How should innovations in organizational design and information technology be adapted to the histories, priorities, and circumstances of firms in different industries? The answers to these questions will determine the future role of the marketing function.

The Emergence of Hybrid Organizations

Traditionally, most firms have been *vertically* structured around functions or departments. Decisions and activities are controlled by a well-defined hierarchy, both within the individual functions and collectively from the top down by senior management. The strength of a vertical organization is functional excellence. It works well when technical expertise is key to competitive success, or when production is high volume and standardized with dedicated, inflexible machinery and systems. The weakness of a vertical organization is coordination. Functions are prone to optimize their own activities, according to their objectives, but not talk to each other in a systematic way. The result is a lack of integrity in products, slow response times, and inflexibility during periods of rapid change.

A *horizontal* or process-oriented organization structures the firm around a small number of strategically important processes or work flows, such as new product development or order generation and fulfilment (Hammer 1996). Each process is comprised of a sequence of activities that are implemented by multidisciplinary teams. Teams are accountable for external objectives such as customers' satisfaction with the outcome of the process, or performance related to competitive benchmarks such as order-processing time. Information is readily available to all team members, unfiltered by a hierarchy or intermediaries.

A distinguishing feature of the horizontal or process-oriented organization is the creation of new managerial roles. Gone are the familiar titles of department manager, section leader, director, and supervisor. In their places we find:

> ➤ *Process owners* who ensure the process is efficiently designed, oversee the day-to-day activities of the team, and have ultimate responsibility for performance

> ➤ *Coaches* with responsibility for maintaining skills and developing specialized talent in each area of necessary expertise. They are the gateway by which new practices and procedures are introduced through educational and expertise-sharing opportunities.

> ➤ *Leaders* who set the strategic direction and provide an integrating logic so the processes can work together effectively. They exercise their leadership through direct interaction and personal example.

Horizontal structures have several other distinguishing features, according to proponents. First, there are fewer layers, because there are fewer supervisory responsibilities in self-managed teams, and only a lean top management is needed to provide direction. Second, there is an emphasis on developing competitively superior capabilities—the complex bundles of skills and accumulated knowledge that enable superior coordination of the activities in the process (Day 1994). Third, core processes and the associated capabilities are determined by the strategy for delivering superior value to customers. Finally, the organization is capable of being continually reconfigured as conditions change, rather than remaining static and rigid.

Most firms are not willing or able to shift to a purely horizontal form; they need to foster vertical skills and disciplines such as the engineering skill to design ergonomically sound products, the financial skills and experience to create the financial services that differentiate GE Capital from its competitors, or the mastery of information technology that enables the seamless integration of a business and its customers. And despite the ambitious claims of the process engineers, there will always be internal handoffs, whether from research to product development or from the center to the field organization.

Hybrid structures combine the horizontal business processes with integrating and specialist functions. Integrating functions such as marketing, strategy development, and human resource management provide the mechanisms for coordinating and allocating resources to the core processes. Specialist functions such as R&D and marketing are needed to provide technical expertise and replenish the horizontal processes with new ideas—either through new insights from outside the firm or the transfer of learning across teams. As a result, most firms start with "centers of excellence" based on traditional departments and disciplines, then modify the vertical function so it is more meaningful. Thus, sales might become customer interaction and engineering could be technical design. The coach—who was once a functional manager—continues to play a central role.

A recent survey of 73 companies found that none were operating with true horizontal structures, but only 32 percent had retained a traditional functional design.[3] Of the others, 38 percent were laying process structures over their functional groups, usually by deploying functional specialists in project teams for specific projects of limited duration, and 30 percent were trying process structures with functional overlays.

A number of consumer packaged goods firms are experimenting with hybrid designs using integrators and specialists as building blocks (George, Freeling, and Court 1994; see also *The Economist* 1994; Low and Fullerton 1994) This path will eventually lead to an organization structure something like that seen in Figure 1. Here, teams are organized around three core processes: the consumer management team, replacing the brand management function, is responsible for customer segments; customer process teams, replacing the sales function, serve the retail accounts; and the supply management team, absorbing the logistics function, ensures on-time delivery to retailers. There is also a strategic integration team, to develop effective overall strategies and coordinate the teams. Although this team relies on deep understanding of the market, it might not be in the marketing function. While functions remain, their roles are to coordinate activities across teams to ensure that shared learning takes place, to acquire and nurture specialized skills, to deploy specialists to the cross-functional process teams, and to achieve scale economies.

These hybrid forms should not be confused with traditional product management approaches, where coordination was the responsibility of brand or product managers who were ostensibly mini-general managers. In reality, these managers were clearly located in marketing and their mandate was to deploy the elements of the marketing mix to protect a brand franchise, with little attention to other functions or activities in the value chain. Because these brand or product managers

---

3. *The study was conducted by the Boston Consulting Group, and reported in* Vision of the Future: Role of Human Resources in the New Corporate Headquarters *(1995),* Washington, DC: The Advisory Board Company.

Figure 1. Packaged Goods Organization—One Possible Approach

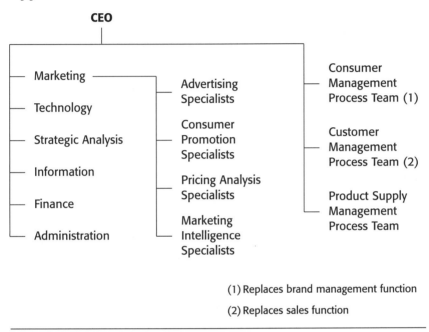

(1) Replaces brand management function

(2) Replaces sales function

Source: McKinsey & Co.

were usually relatively junior they lacked authority, resources, or willingness to initiate cross-organizational activities such as partnering with channel members or undertaking joint promotions.

However, the absence of brand managers raises the question of who will manage the brand asset to ensure there is proper reinvestment to protect, enhance, and realize its value. One approach is to create a separate brand development team, with specialist skills to manage critical components such as trademark protection and sponsorships and to coordinate the overall flow of brand information (Hill, Newkirk, and Henderson 1995). In short, these and other tasks of the brand manager will not disappear; they will be accomplished in a more responsive and integrated fashion.

Impediments to Organizational Changes

Although the horizontal or hybrid structure, with core processes closely aligned to a strategy of delivering superior value, is an appealing concept, it is unlikely that most firms will be able to implement it effectively.

Some firms will be captives of their past, with structures and cultures that are simply too divergent from the hybrid firm. Here, the forces of inertia are so powerful that management is unable to muster the energy to change, and entrenched functions resist the dilution of their power and privilege. In fact, these functions can mobilize a powerful coalition to maintain the status quo. Kmart, for example, was unwilling and unable to change a costly system of regional headquarters—with extensive duplication of head-office control and merchandising functions—to adopt the more streamlined and centralized approach of Wal-Mart. This resistance was no doubt rooted in an unwillingness to share information freely throughout the company because the control of vital information is an important basis of power and status. Yet rapid and widespread dissemination of market information is absolutely critical to a market-driven organization.

In such cases, where resistance to change is great, response to changing market requirements may be limited to piecemeal tinkering at the margin. The result is a proliferation of organizational positions to address immediate problems, with overlaps in responsibility that reduce the clarity of roles. In recent years, for example, firms have added category managers, segment managers, key account managers, area managers, and trade managers, often without any revision of adjacent roles.

Other firms will find the need for a horizontal process-oriented structure so compelling that they will attempt the transformation, but fall short, a victim of all the difficulties encountered by TQM and process re-engineering: lack of sustained top management commitment, impatience, and a poor understanding of the underlying principles. Despite an avowed interest in satisfying customers, these efforts tend to be internally focused on self-contained processes (Kordupleski, Rust, and Zahorik 1993).

For example, seldom does a process re-engineering effort tackle more than two or three processes, each chosen because of its strategic centrality, the presence of a committed and capable sponsor, and a favorable history of change (Davenport 1993). However, even if these individual processes have been optimized, they won't necessarily come together as an optimized whole (Leemon 1993). The missing ingredient is an integrating strategic logic. This logic should be driven by *marketing* considerations such as: (1) who are the *target customers?* (so that the teams managing individual processes can select customers to nurture or discourage based on profitability or opportunities for growth); (2) what *values* are the target customers seeking? (so that appropriate trade-offs can be made on features and benefits); (3) how will *competitive advantage* be gained? (so timely moves that disadvantage competitors can be made), and (4) how will the target customers be reached and served? In other words, effective integration across processes requires readily available market information, shared assumptions, and a coherent strategy that relates short-run tactical moves to long-run profit and growth objectives.

How Information Technology Enables Organization Change

Although the hybrid, process-oriented organization requires big changes in mindset and organizational assumptions, it is only made feasible by advances in information technology. Corporate data networks permit firms to link internal teams for better, faster decision making, and to "unbundle" their business systems to focus on the promising parts of their traditionally integrated businesses.

These data network capabilities are also at the heart of interactive marketing strategies that allow dialogue and collaboration with customers and consumers. But strategies that are more interactive require organizations that are more flexible and decentralized than traditional hierarchies. The usual alignment of roles, in which the product marketing function controls information flows and passes marketing plans and programs to sales and service support, is too confusing and time consuming when the firm must be able to customize product/service packages for increasingly diverse and fast-changing customer segments.

The essence of interactive marketing is the use of information *from* the customer rather than *about* the customer. Firms selling large capital equipment to a few sophisticated buyers—manufacturers of aircraft engines, digital switchgear, or packaging machinery, for example—already have close collaborative relationships with their customers. However, interactivity is a radical departure—with exhilarating and potentially threatening prospects—for firms such as financial or travel services, publishing, apparel, or white goods that have traditionally used broadcast marketing (mass media and intermediaries) to reach large segments of the population.

Aligning the Structure with the Interactive Strategy

As a firm's strategy becomes more interactive, there must be greater dispersion of information and decision making throughout the organization to ensure maintenance of alignment. Here, structure both follows and enables strategy.

The least interactive configuration is the traditional broadcast marketing strategy, using mass media and intermediaries to reach large market segments, which is well aligned with the traditional functional organization. As the strategy is augmented with interactive elements or becomes completely interactive, an organizational transformation is needed.

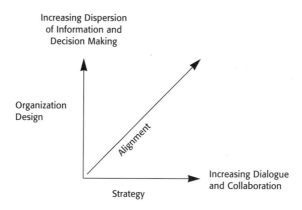

Increasing Dispersion
of Information and
Decision Making

Organization
Design

Alignment

Strategy

Increasing Dialogue
and Collaboration

Augmented Strategies. Most organizations will not adopt completely interactive strategies. They may, for example, simply augment traditional media and methods with interactive media by putting existing
materials on the Web site. More substantial departures involve continuity and retention activities, such as frequent flyer programs or
micro-marketing, which employs store-by-store or zip-code-by-zip-
code distinctions between marketing programs. These augmentations
can be implemented by grafting the following components to a traditional or hybrid organization:

➤ Customer segment managers who have responsibility for
  designing tailored communications or micro-marketing
  programs

➤ Technology support groups that provide an in-house
  capability to develop Web sites, support a continuity
  program, or experiment with interactive media. These
  could be housed in the marketing services or information system group.

➤ Outsourcing of specialist skills in areas such as usage
  tracking, or creative programming of interfaces

➤ *Ad hoc* multifunctional teams (with guidance from a senior steering group) for more ambitious programs such as data-based marketing where tailored messages or catalogs are sent to individuals based on their profiles of interests and activities

Fully Interactive Strategies. A simple augmentation does not take full advantage of the opportunity to repeatedly address customers as individuals in light of what has been learned from their previous responses. To exploit this capability, a transformed organization design is required.

Examples of fully interactive strategies are shown in Figure 2. They include mass customization, virtual stores, and collaborative learning to fit services to needs, which was pioneered by Individual Inc. and practiced effectively by USAA. Also included here are the approaches to business partnering used by Astra Merck and channel linking such as the Procter & Gamble and Wal-Mart partnership.

These strategies are distinguished from augmentation approaches by the barriers to imitation they create; the impediments and road-blocks faced by firms using traditional or even augmented strategies as they try to emulate a competitor who is fully interactive. For example, a traditional pharmaceutical company or an industrial equipment firm selling from a catalog will not be able to match the customer-responsiveness of an Astra Merck or a mass customizer. The differences in strategy, structure, systems, and skills are simply too great to bridge. Faced with such impediments, an established firm will have to transform itself with a completely new organization design or set up an independent unit with a responsive structure.

Appropriate Alignment. An independent unit is most desirable when (1) interactive marketing represents a large potential opportunity, (2) there is likely to be significant conflict with existing channels, (3) there are large culture, skill, and process differences between the established organization and the new unit, and (4) the existing organization cannot accommodate the need for cross-functional integra-

Figure 2. Aligning Strategy with Structure

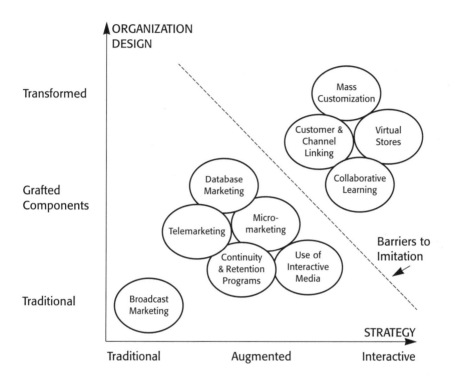

tion (Parsons, Zeisser, and Waitman 1996). What, then, is the appropriate alignment for an independent customer-responsive unit within an organization: should it be housed in a distinct unit that is part of an existing organization, physically located in a different place, and/or have its own funding and accounting?

The appropriate structure for these distinct units will exploit data networks to manage the necessary dispersion of information and decision making, thereby altering organization structures in two ways. First, the trend to outsourcing will accelerate. With distributed low-cost networks, it is becoming cheaper and more effective to communicate between firms than to develop or maintain specialist skills in-house. Second, teams, functional specialists, and project groups will increasingly be linked to make better and faster collective decisions. The outcome will be an advanced version of the hybrid organization called the *hypertext firm*.

Hypertext Organizations. This design envisions an organization of interconnected layers, as shown in Figure 3 (Nonaka and Takeuchi 1995). It is analogous to the layers in a hypertext computer program that enable one to drill below a text for greater detail and amplification. On top is a process-team layer; here teams manage horizontal processes or engage in knowledge-creating activities such as new product development or charting a new interactive strategy. The team members are assigned from diverse functions or practice areas for the duration of the project, or, in the case of core processes, they might have a continuing commitment with the option of returning to a functional home.

Figure 3. Hypertext Organizations

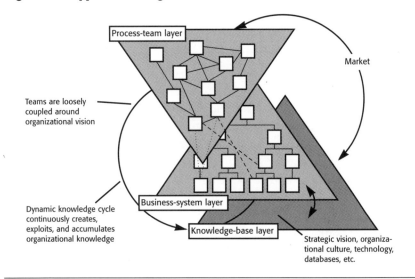

Source: Nonaka and Takeuchi (1995)

In the middle is the functionally structured business-system layer that develops the expertise to support the business strategy and provides a talent pool for the functional teams. This layer also creates opportunities for networking and sharing functional expertise so learning is readily available to all teams. Where particular skills are needed by many teams, such as the design and sourcing of marketing research studies, the specialist with this knowledge may be permanently housed on this layer. These business systems are linked to each other and the business processes by information technology, rather than by a traditional command and control system.

The foundation is the "knowledge-base" layer where cumulative organizational knowledge resides. This is not an identifiable organizational form; it is composed of both the tacit knowledge found in the corporate vision and culture, and the explicit knowledge found within the information systems. Members of the hypertext organization can readily shift from one layer to another as circumstances change. However, someone belongs or reports to only one unit at a time, in contrast to the matrix structure where it is possible to belong to two units at the same time.

Regardless of how the organization is designed, it will require a fluid structure that is able to respond quickly to shifts in strategy and to act on new knowledge. In a process-oriented structure such as the hypertext form, this is achieved by having each of the processes tightly focused on customer value.

Aligning Strategies, Capabilities, and Processes in Hybrid Organizations

A hybrid design has many possible variants. These will be manifested in the relative importance of staff groups, functional specialists, and process or project teams, as well as in the choice of core processes, and the coordinating mechanisms that tie the elements together. Each of these design choices will depend on the unique requirements and circumstances of the firm and its strategy within the industry. An organizational design that works for the health care products division of Unilever will not serve the health insurance business of Metropolitan Life or the computer printer group at Hewlett-Packard. Yet each of these organizations may profitably borrow features from the others. Thus, General Motors has brought in brand managers from consumer packaged goods firms to bring greater clarity to the muddied images of brands like Oldsmobile, Buick, and Chevrolet. (In the meantime, of course, the brand management model is in trouble in many packaged goods firms because their environment has changed.)

The particular form that any hybrid organization assumes emerges from a complex interplay among many forces. First, industry character determines which skills and assets are most crucial to competitive success. Within an industry context, there will be a variety of strategies for delivering superior customer value. There are also constraints imposed by resource limitations, inertia from commitments to the status quo, and the good or bad experience of previous organizational experiments.

Industry Character

Industries can be classified according to the resources that are the dominant features of their competitive landscape and command the greatest attention from managers. The scale of investments in these resources, and the ability to excel in the management of the core processes that utilize these investments, determine a firm's performance.

One typology distinguishes industries according to the relative influence of three resources: (1) capacity, (2) brands or customer relationships, (3) knowledge and innovation processes.[4]

---

4. *From Miles, Snow, and Sharfman (1993). The typology of industries derived from their measures of variety is described in Collis and Ghemawat (1994).*

Capacity-dominated Industries. Here, participation requires competitors to make relatively large investments in the fixed capacity of their plants or networks. Typically they spend small proportions of their sales on marketing or R&D. Prototypical industries are basic fibers and chemicals, steel, and pulp and paper, which have high ratios of assets to sales, often exceeding two to one.

Because capacity utilization and operational efficiency are so critical, and because standardization of processes to get high throughput results in relatively undifferentiated products, competition for the necessary volume emphasizes price. Only when all players are operating close to their capacity limits do price pressures abate.

Because resource commitments are so large, and competitive moves are highly visible and quickly matched, market shares tend to be stable. Profit differences between firms usually reflect differences in scale, operating efficiency, and input costs. Occasionally a competitor such as Nucor, which pioneered mini-mills for steel making, will commit to a new manufacturing process or format that reduces costs markedly, but in general emphasis is on incremental improvements in process efficiency.

Customer-driven Industries. Most important in these industries is the ability to maintain close and loyal relationships with customers and build strong brand names, for these are the resources that are the most difficult for competitors to match. These resources assume prominence in industries in which there are abundant opportunities for differentiation of products or services, and in which the customers buy frequently and are fragmented into numerous segments with diverse requirements. These include food and beverages, personal care products, household durables, and financial services.

Heavy investments in advertising, marketing, and product development programs are required to create awareness, reinforce attitudes, and encourage repeat purchases. Profit differences stem mostly from differences in perceived quality, scale-related differences in market coverage, and the strength of brand name equity. There is also intense competition on other factors, including production efficiency and logistics, but these are more readily copied by competitors.

Knowledge-focused Industries. In these industries, investments in innovation (and specifically R&D) account for a disproportionately large share of the value-added, and the firm's most valuable assets are the patents and cumulative skills and knowledge of its employees. While all firms have deep knowledge bases, these industries stand out in their focus on knowledge and the ability to produce streams of unique products or innovative processes. Exemplars are pharmaceutical drugs, computers, software, and entertainment industries. As a rule, these industries are less mature, and competitive processes tend to be very dynamic, so market shares are unstable.

Some industries are a blend of several types. In addition, over time, some industries may change their characteristics and evolve from one type to another. Nonetheless, the differences in the investment profiles at any point in time help explain the priorities and preoccupations of managers, and shape their choices of strategy, capabilities, and organizational structure.

Strategies and Capabilities

Within an industry, there are as many strategies as firms. However, industry character has a strong steering influence on the menu of strategy choices and dictates the natural strategy that most firms will follow. This congruency can be seen by comparing the three industry types with a typology of strategies based on three distinct ways of delivering superior customer value (Treacy and Wiersema 1995).

Each of the three "value disciplines" differs in its central value proposition and the capabilities it requires. Every business acquires many capabilities that enable it to move its products through the value chain. Only a few of these need to be superior to competition. These are the distinctive capabilities that support a value proposition that is valuable to customers and hard for competitors to match.

A basic premise of the three value disciplines is that it is not possible to be all things to all customers. Once an initial core of common customer requirements is satisfied—and firms are less able to favorably differentiate themselves on these requirements—their interests will begin to diverge. One customer group emphasizes higher performance, another is willing to trade off the latest in performance for low prices and dependability, and a third values quality of relationships, trust, personalized services, and advice when choosing a supplier. Each value strategy excels at meeting the distinctive needs of one segment, while offering parity or competitively acceptable performance on the attributes that are less important. Thus, each strategy requires different capabilities, and these in turn dictate the organizational arrangements.

Operational Excellence. The key to this strategy is the provision of consistent quality at the best price, with a standardized business system that minimizes customer cost and difficulty in acquiring or using the product. The leaders with this strategy invest heavily in integrated low-cost transaction-handling systems, and minimize intermediate processing steps. Their dominant position in the market enhances bargaining power with suppliers. Exemplars are Wal-Mart, Marriott, Southwest Airlines, and McDonald's.

Mastery of this strategy requires an organization dedicated to the consistent execution of the core processes of order fulfillment, supply chain management, logistics, service delivery, and transaction processing.

Standardization of processes and integration of activities across organizational boundaries requires top-down management systems and well-defined operating procedures. While employees can take initiative within these organizations they are more directed than enabled.

Customer Responsiveness. This strategy emphasizes the careful tailoring and adaptation of products and services to increasingly finer and more precise customer requirements. There is a strong orientation toward identifying the distinct needs of individual customers or micro-segments, in order to nurture long-term relationships with customers. A "have it your way" mindset prevails.

The core processes to support this strategy are flexible and facilitate multiple modes of producing and delivering products and services: market segmentation and market needs analysis, client acquisition and retention, service delivery, and customization of pricing, features, and service levels.

Such firms are masters of "mass customization" and other interactive strategies. In contrast to operationally excellent companies they empower front-line sales and service teams to make decisions close to the customers and adapt procedures to changing circumstances.

Performance Superiority. A firm pursuing this strategy delivers customer value through a continuous flow of innovative products and services that push the state of the art of the fashion or technology or provide useful new applications of existing products or services. Such companies are open to new ideas, sensitive to latent customer needs, successful at exploring and integrating streams of new technologies, and effective at mobilizing resources to pursue these opportunities. The core processes they have mastered include: market sensing, fast-paced product development and launch, technology integration, and flexible manufacturing (that can adapt quickly to new requirements, although it may not be good at mass customization).

Processes are managed with a decentralized, team-oriented, and loose-knit structure. An exemplar is Hewlett-Packard's three computer printer divisions, which have come to dominate their home and office markets with technology advances, sustained by a rapid fire of product variations, price cuts, and willingness to attack competitors.

Another example is General Electric Medical Systems, which achieves performance superiority in the medical diagnostic imaging market (including X rays, CAT scanners, and Magnetic Resonance Imaging devices) through five core processes. The advanced technology process and offerings development process are focused on tomorrow's customers. The go-to-market (identification of market needs and fine-tuning of designs to meet them), order-to-remittance (which starts with the placement of the order and ends with delivery of the equipment), and service delivery processes serve the current customers, while the support activities serve the other processes.

Alignment of Value Strategy and Industry Character

As the alignment matrix in Figure 4 demonstrates, there is a good deal of congruency between the three value strategies and the three characteristic industries. When the dominant resource is capacity, the natural strategy is operational excellence, whereas firms in knowledge-focused industries gravitate to a performance superiority value proposition, and customer-driven industries emphasize customer responsiveness.

However, it is important to note that the three value strategies are not necessarily incompatible, and that it is possible to pursue value leadership along more than one type of advantage. This usually happens when a firm has preferential access to resources, or when competitors are blocked from copying. In addition, in the absence of a major discontinuity in the market, there will be an inexorable narrowing of the differences among competitors pursuing the same natural strategy. It then becomes advantageous for some firms to seek leadership with strategies that diverge from the diagonal. This must be done while maintaining competitive parity with the natural strategy, which now becomes the price of admission to the industry. Thus, in a capacity-driven industry like pulp and paper, efficiency of operations and productivity continue to be a priority; however, when the major players have all achieved the same level of efficiency, the customer needs a new reason to choose among the contenders. Whether

Figure 4. The Congruence of Value Strategies and Industry Character

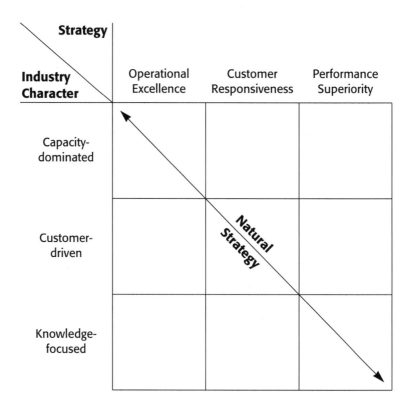

this is feasible or desirable depends on the ease with which competitors can match the new thrust, and on whether the differences between customer groups have become sufficiently large to justify the investment in a new value proposition.

What Role for Marketing?

As organizations evolve toward hybrid structures, using self-directed process teams with well-defined external objectives to accomplish much of the firm's work, the importance of all functional departments will inevitably be diminished. Nonetheless, some functions will be relatively more powerful than others—that is, they will control more resources and have more influence in the strategy dialogue. Will marketing be the lead function, rather than operations, sales, finance, engineering, or technology? That depends on the answers to these questions:

1. How influential is the marketing function in the current organization? Is the culture supportive of a dominant role for the marketing function?

2. Has the organization been able to successfully make the transition from a vertical, functional, or matrix structure, to a hybrid or hypertext structure? Are the constraints to making this transition likely to be overcome by the pressures of change?

3. What are the core processes, and what is the contribution of the marketing function to the direction and integration of these processes?

The eventual role of the marketing function will also be influenced by its current status in the organization. Useful indications are the influence of marketers in the strategy dialogue, the reliance of decision makers on market intelligence, as well as size of budget and head-count. The functional background of the top management team and their direct experience with marketing activities offer additional clues.

However, in the long run what matters more is culture—the basic set of values and beliefs shared through the organization that provides norms for appropriate behavior and helps the members understand the priorities of the organization (Webster 1994). The role of marketing will be strong in an organization that puts the customer's interest first, and defines each job in terms of its contribution to the delivery of superior customer value. In a strong sales, technology, or internally oriented culture these interests will be subordinated, and marketing's role will be weaker. The consequences of these cultural differences are pervasive, ranging from the extent of interfunctional coordination, the focus of control for projects, the availability of market intelligence throughout the organization, and the types of incentives.[5]

Alternative Marketing Roles

The future role of the marketing function will also depend on whether the structure evolves toward a strategically integrated, hybrid structure. This, in turn, depends on the prevailing satisfaction or frustration with the existing structure, the urgency for change to cope with new circumstances, and the ability of the organization to overcome the barriers to change. If no significant change is made, and marketing is already the lead function, then the future organization might be described as a *functional fiefdom*. If the organization successfully implements a hybrid structure with a strong process orientation, marketing may become a *central guidance* or *subordinate function*.

Functional Fiefdom. Here the marketing function has historically been separate and aloof. It is likely to be the lead function because the industry is customer driven, and power is enhanced by controlling access to market information. Its lead role will persist as long as the organization retains a traditional functional or product management structure, or external trends don't cause the balance of power in the organization to shift. However, in markets where the prices and products can be customized at the point of contact with the customer, new approaches will be required so that marketing programs can be launched independently by those closest to the market. In addition, in packaged goods firms the pressure to respond faster and

---

5. *There is a growing body of research on the consequences of cultural differences, including Kohli and Jaworski (1990), and Deshpandé, Farley, and Webster (1993).*

better to the demands of retailers will enhance the power of the sales and logistics functions.

Subordinate Function. This outcome is most likely for firms in capacity-driven or knowledge-focused industries where the organization structure has evolved into a hybrid form. Marketing people are likely to occupy a subordinate role in sales support activities or as participants in core process teams. This outcome is especially likely when the culture is very engineering or technology driven, and marketing's role is simply to implement tactical merchandising programs.[6] Many of the specialist marketing activities are likely to be outsourced.

Central Guidance Function. It is increasingly apparent that most companies will not be well served if they continue with a rigidly functionalized organization—even if marketing is the lead function—or if they subordinate marketing within a horizontal process-oriented structure. Market leadership will be attained only when a strong marketing orientation pervades both the culture and the organization structure. This central guidance function means that marketing, as a functional unit or integrated into the top management team in the business planning function, takes responsibility for:

> *Articulation,* by defining and renewing the value proposition and positioning in the market, and specifying the mechanisms for taking the product or service to the market

> *Navigation,* through effective market sensing and sharing of market information, opportunity identification, and performance measurement

> *Orchestration,* by providing the essential "glue" for a coherent, market-driven whole

This central guidance role will be enhanced when the core processes depend on the ability to: (1) collect, interpret, and disseminate infor-

---

6. *These are vividly described in Workman (1993) and Virden (1995).*

mation about the market, (2) manage close linkages with end-consumers and channel partners to maximize retention and loyalty, (3) choose target segments and adapt the value proposition to their changing requirements and competitive moves, and (4) nurture and exploit brand equity. In fact, in the hypercompetitive markets of the next millennium, these capabilities will be increasingly important for *all* firms.

Summary

Why have organizational design issues come to be central to our thinking about the future of marketing? How are firms redesigning their strategies, structures, and processes, and what are the implications for marketing as an organizational orientation, functional specialty, and general management responsibility?

The overriding answer is that firms have learned that success comes only when their organizations are truly market driven—with a mission to create superior value for their customers. This requires an ability to execute a well-focused strategy, while continuously adapting core processes, skills, and activities to keep them in alignment with changing market opportunities and customer requirements.

Firms have also learned that the ideal of a continuously adaptive organization is close to being realized. Information technology and new approaches to organization design, along with sharp challenges to the restrictions of the traditional functional design, have led to an unprecedented era of organization innovation. Now it is the customer that drives the organization—not the other way around. Or, as one 3M manager put it:

> The fact that we are a
>   multi-dimensional
>   multi-functional
>   multi-regional
>   multi-plant organization
> is not the customer's fault.

Underlying this fundamental reorientation are four premises that I have developed in this chapter:

1. Firms will increasingly evolve toward a hybrid or hypertext form of organization—combining the best features of horizontal process and vertical functional forms—in order to get closer to their customers.

2. There will be a great deal of variety in hybrid designs that are adopted, depending on the alignment of the value strategy and the core capabilities that are exercised in the processes. This will dictate the relative importance of staff groups, function specialists, and process teams.

3. Advances in data networks will permit firms to link internal teams for better, faster decision making, and to devise more interactive strategies that use information *from* the customer rather than *about* the customer.

4. As strategies become more interactive, leading to increasing dialogue and collaboration with customers and channels, there must be greater dispersion of information and decision making throughout the organization.

Marketing will play several roles in these hybrid organizations. As an organizational orientation, it provides the cultural beliefs and norms that ensure the primacy of the customer's interest in all activities. As a general management responsibility, it defines and articulates the value strategy, provides navigation aids through the fast-changing market environment, and provides the rationale for orchestrating and integrating the collection of organization processes. As a functional specialty, it provides the expertise in market sensing and customer linking needed by the process teams to ensure they are closely aligned with the market. ∎

Part III

➤ ➤ ➤ ➤ ➤ ➤ ➤

Preparing for the Future

➤ 5

Future Prospects for Marketing Education

Robert D. Buzzell
Rajendra Sisodia

During the 1990s, management education, including marketing, has undergone its most far-reaching reappraisal since the early 1960s. The quality and relevance of courses, teaching methods, and research agendas have all been called into question. At the same time, as noted elsewhere in this volume, marketing practices and institutions have been dramatically affected by the globalization of competition, advances in information and communication technology, the "re-engineering" of business processes, and other factors. This has created another set of pressures for change since business school courses and research programs must reflect these changes in marketing practices and systems.

In the first section of this paper, we review the forces affecting management education during the 1990s, with special attention to marketing. Our discussion focuses primarily on marketing education in the United States, although many of the same trends apply to programs elsewhere in the world. We focus almost exclusively on M.B.A. and other graduate degree programs, because these programs are considered the most important in the field of business education, and have also received the most widespread criticism in recent years.

The second section of the paper deals with recent changes in graduate management education. This section is based in part on a survey of university management education programs carried out by mail and telephone in mid-1995. We sent questionnaires, and made follow-up telephone calls, to 40 schools with M.B.A. programs ranked highest by the 1994 *Business Week* survey (Byrne and Bongiorno 1994). We also included in the survey several other schools that had made especially innovative changes in their programs. The survey requested information on recent changes in the M.B.A. curriculum and, more specifically, marketing courses. We received reasonably complete replies from 18 schools, including most of those ranked as the 10 leaders in the *Business Week* survey.

In the final section of the paper we explore prospects for change in marketing education during the late 1990s and the first decade of the 21st century.

The Crisis in Management Education

After almost three decades of steady growth, graduate-level management education programs are being critically evaluated and, in many cases, dramatically redesigned. As one observer put it, "Business education's current plunge into self-analysis is the deepest in 30 years" (O'Reilly 1994). A 1990 report commissioned by the Graduate Management Admissions Council called for a "fundamental rethinking of graduate management education" (Commission on Admission to Graduate Management Education 1990).

Maturing of the "Business School Industry"

Discussion of the product life cycle is a staple in basic marketing courses, but the concept has rarely been applied to business education as a "product." In fact, however, the historical trends in M.B.A. enrollments have followed the classic "S-curve" life cycle pattern that has been observed in many industries.

Prior to 1960, only about 5,000 M.B.A. degrees were awarded annually by American universities, and M.B.A. programs were virtually unknown elsewhere in the world. Beginning in the mid-1960s, enrollment in M.B.A. programs began a period of growth that lasted into the early 1990s.

The number of master's degrees in business grew from around 25,000 in 1970 to 55,000 in 1980 and 80,000 in 1992. The highest rate of growth came in the 1970s, when M.B.A. enrollments increased at an average annual rate of 10 percent; the growth rate was considerably lower in the 1980s, averaging 3.5 percent per year (Snyder 1993). Between 1990 and 1993, the number of students taking the Graduate Management Aptitude Test (GMAT) declined by 20 percent, prompting widespread concern about the future of business education.

The growth in M.B.A. enrollments was fueled by several demographic and social trends:

> The first of the baby boomers—those born in the late 1940s—began reaching their 20s in the mid-1960s. The number of men and women aged 25-34, prime years for M.B.A. program attendance, grew from 25 million in 1970 to 37 million in 1980 and more than 43 million in 1990.

> Average educational attainment levels rose sharply: in 1960, fewer than 8 percent of people aged 25 or older had completed four years of college or more. By 1993 the figure was almost 22 percent. Holding a bachelor's degree, once a mark of some distinction, became commonplace in many segments of society, particularly among those aspiring to management careers.

> Female participation in the labor force grew rapidly, from around 38 percent of those 16 years or older in 1960 to 58 percent in 1993. This contributed to increased demand for management education among women, who represented

only 4 percent of all master's degrees awarded in 1971 but 35 percent in 1991.

The growth in demand for graduate business education during the 1970s and 1980s attracted many new university "suppliers" to enter the field. In the United States, the number of M.B.A. programs rose from about 300 in 1970 to 700 in 1995. In Europe, an estimated 400 M.B.A. programs competed for applicants by 1995, almost all of them established since 1970. Growth in the number of programs, especially part-time ones, attracted more students into the field, just as increased availability of a product typically stimulates increased sales.

The maturing of the graduate business education "industry," coupled with reductions in federal and state support for higher education since 1990, has meant that M.B.A. programs must compete for students and resources. Like competing businesses in a mature industry, schools have pursued a variety of strategies aimed at quality improvement, product differentiation, and pricing.

Quality and Relevance

The rapid expansion of graduate business education during the 1970s and 1980s led, inevitably, to variability in program quality. Retiring Harvard Business School Dean John McArthur provoked a lively controversy by suggesting, in a mid-1995 interview, that ease of entry and lack of meaningful standards had led to declining average quality for M.B.A. degrees. Some other business school deans strongly disagreed with McArthur's views (*Business and Society Review* 1995).

Concerns about the quality of business education were intensified by the publicity surrounding two published rankings of leading M.B.A. programs introduced during the 1980s by *Business Week* and *U.S. News & World Report* (Gales 1995). As these rankings attracted greater attention, even minor changes in a school's ranking from one year to the next stimulated widespread debate and, often, intensified efforts by faculty and administrators to exploit favorable comments or explain away critical ones. Although there have been a number of methodological criticisms of these published rankings, the annual surveys have clearly heightened awareness and concern about program quality among potential applicants and prospective employers alike.

In addition to the overall quality of graduate business programs, concerns about the *relevance* of many programs' content to management practice have grown since the 1980s. One frequent criticism is that business school faculty members devote too much time to "purely academic" research and publication in academic journals, and too little to issues of real interest to practicing managers. Ironically, the faculty emphasis on rigorous, peer-reviewed research publication can be traced in large part to the last widespread reappraisal of business education in the late 1950s. At that time, two influential foundation-sponsored reports on the state of business education advocated increased research effort and more rigorous research methods for business school faculties (Gordon and Howell 1959; Pierson 1959). Their intent was to improve the academic quality of business education programs. According to some critics, they succeeded all too well, but at the cost of diminished practical relevance (see, for example, Elliott et al. 1994; Stanton 1988).

Related to concerns about the relevance of business school faculty research is the perception that schools put too much emphasis on quantitative methods and other formal analytical tools. As a result, some observers feel, M.B.A. graduates are prone to "analysis paralysis" and are reluctant to undertake major innovations (Behrman and Levin 1984).

In addition, even the highest-ranked programs are structured in such a way as to perpetuate the functional mentality that many companies have sought to overcome in recent years. According to this line of criticism, the "functional silos" that exist in real-world organizations are mirrored in "ivory silos" in academe (Linder and Smith 1992; *Harvard Business Review* 1992). Thus, a sequence of courses in marketing may be largely separate from, and independent of, parallel courses in operations management and finance. The result is that when M.B.A. graduates begin their careers they must re-learn, or perhaps even un-learn, much of what they have studied in traditional programs.

Other Trends Affecting Management Education

Other factors affecting business education include the increasing diversity of students, growing pressure to contain costs, and increased competition from nonuniversity educational programs.

Diversity of Students. Students enrolled today in business education programs, both graduate and undergraduate, are clearly more diverse than their predecessors. Of special importance, they are typically older and have more work experience. As a result they are more familiar (although often in a superficial way) with marketing concepts and practices. An example illustrates the point: on the first day of class, a student in an introductory marketing course taught by one of the authors cited an article on pricing that had appeared in the *Harvard Business Review* only a week earlier. It turned out that the student had worked as a research assistant at a major consulting firm where the authors of the article were employed.

The fastest-growing category of business school students (and of university students in general) is those aged 25 and older. Since most of these students are employed, they attend classes on a part-time basis. As a result, part-timers accounted for an estimated two-thirds of all M.B.A. students in the mid-1990s (McGinn 1995).

Another dimension of diversity is national origin. Since the 1980s, a growing proportion of students enrolled in American business education programs, especially at the graduate level, have been from other countries. This creates both opportunities and problems: classroom discussions can be enriched by the greater diversity of student backgrounds and experiences. On the other hand, one cannot assume common knowledge of such things as products, brand names, and types of retail outlets.

Cost Constraints. Many business schools came under increasing pressure during the late 1980s and early 1990s to contain their operating costs. One result has been a marked increase in the use of part-time "adjunct" instructors, who provide instruction at significantly lower cost than tenure-track faculty. In many cases adjunct instructors are excellent teachers who contribute to greater real-world relevance in M.B.A. programs. But increased reliance on part-time instructors has also contributed to concern about the quality of some M.B.A. programs.

Competition. Concerns about the quality and relevance of university-based business education programs have prompted an increasing number of companies to develop in-house educational programs (Watson 1995). Most in-house offerings feature short programs on specific topics such as sales management; some, however, more closely resemble full-fledged M.B.A. programs. A prominent example of the latter is the master of science in management program offered by Arthur D. Little. This program has been in operation since 1964, but was positioned more directly in competition with university programs when the firm applied for M.B.A. degree accreditation by the AACSB (American Assembly of Collegiate Schools of Business) in late 1995 (Arthur D. Little, Inc. 1996). Another source of competition for university-based programs is the Keller Graduate School of Management (self-styled as "America's M.B.A.") which, in early 1996, offered a part-time M.B.A. program in 18 locations throughout the United States.

Demand for nondegree executive education has also been growing rapidly in recent years. *Business Week* estimated in 1995 that companies spend nearly $15 billion a year in training programs for managers and professionals. Most of these are short, nondegree programs on specific topics.

Other trends pertinent to executive education are the following:

➤ Courses are becoming more "action-oriented," focusing on solving real problems at companies. They are also being used as part of an orchestrated "change management" process at the initiative, and with the involvement, of senior management. Exemplars of this approach include GE's well-known Management Development Institute in Crotonville, N.Y. and Motorola University. Many business schools are basing their own executive program development efforts on this model.

➤ Related to the above, there is more collaboration between companies and universities to create customized courses. Many schools now derive about half of their executive education revenues from such programs.

➤ Executive education courses are becoming shorter; for example, MIT has discontinued its eight-week program for senior executives.

➤ International students make up an increasing percentage of attendees at leading executive programs, such as Harvard's Advanced Management Program.

Changes in M.B.A. Programs

Responding to the trends described in the preceding section and to other environmental changes, many business schools carried out intensive curriculum reviews during the late 1980s and early 1990s. The ensuing program revisions have generally been aimed at improving quality and relevance. In addition, some schools have pursued strategies of "product differentiation," and a few have even shortened their programs—an approach analogous to price-cutting in a maturing industry.

Changes in Curriculum Structure

At one time the typical M.B.A. curriculum included "core" required courses in just a few basic management functions and skills. Often these included marketing, finance, accounting or control, organizational behavior, and quantitative methods.

During the 1980s and early 1990s many business schools introduced additional core courses in other fields such as management information systems, business ethics, and human resource management. (Operations management and strategic management or business policy were parts of the traditional core in some schools but came as later additions in others.)

The addition of new required courses forced a "downsizing" in the traditional core courses such as marketing management (see Harvard Business School 1993). Thus, the number of class sessions devoted to the required marketing course—which is the only marketing course taken by many students—has been reduced from 40 or more to around 30 in some M.B.A. programs. As a result, there is considerable pressure to use each class meeting and each assignment as productively as possible.

A second change has been the development of cross-functional courses specifically designed to develop students' skills in dealing with issues of coordination within an organization. An example is a course offered by the Wharton School on "New Product Design, Manufacturing, and Marketing," taught by a team of faculty members drawn from marketing and operations management. At some schools, such as Babson College, the University of Tennessee, Case Western Reserve, and the University of Minnesota, substantial portions of the M.B.A. curriculum are now being devoted to cross-functional projects (see AACSB 1995). On a more modest scale, in 1995-96 the required first-year courses in marketing and operations management at the Harvard Business School included a joint segment on new product development and product launch marketing.

Many of the cross-functional courses offered by business schools are built around team projects intended to help students develop the team-building and group decision-making skills that are seen as essential to effective competition in the 1990s. Participation in these cross-functional courses will, it is hoped, provide a better foundation than traditional functionally oriented courses for later involvement in process design or re-engineering projects during the early stages of their careers.

Internationalization

For most business schools a major curriculum change in the 1990s has been greater emphasis on the international aspects of management. Clearly, increased global competition has been one of the main driving forces of change in marketing management practice since the mid-1980s, when marketing practitioners began to face such issues as how to respond to challenges by foreign competitors, how to enter foreign markets, and how to coordinate marketing programs across national markets. Seldom were managers, at least in large American corporations, well prepared to address such problems.

In response, business schools have recently intensified their efforts to prepare their students to manage effectively in a global economy. This development is not entirely new. As long ago as 1978 the AACSB revised its accrediting standards for business schools to include a requirement that curricula should be designed to "prepare students for leadership roles in business and society—domestic and worldwide" (AACSB 1978). Two years later the standards were further revised to include a requirement that every student be "exposed to the international dimension through one or more elements in the curriculum" (AACSB 1980).

While the need for an international perspective in management education has long been recognized, in most business schools implementation of the AACSB requirement has left much to be desired. A 1995 survey article on "the internationalization of the business curriculum" concluded, "Most schools sought only an awareness of the international dimension of business, rather than competence or expertise" (Kaminarides and Roderick 1995). Many schools offer a single required course in international management and attempt to "infuse" increasing amounts of international materials (such as case studies) into traditional courses. In marketing specifically, around three-fourths of master's degree programs offered elective courses in international marketing in the mid-1990s (Kwok, Arpan, and Folks 1994).

Among those faculties that have made more concerted efforts in the international sphere, one approach has been to establish an overseas branch, as the University of Chicago did in Barcelona in 1995. An alternative used by many schools, including Columbia University, has been to establish exchange programs or other types of alliances with foreign schools.

A few schools offer specialized graduate degrees in international management. In 1995 the Thunderbird School of the American Graduate School of International Management celebrated its 50th anniversary as a business school specifically designed to prepare students for careers in international business. A more recent entrant is the University of South Carolina's master of international business degree, which includes a six-month internship at a non-U.S. company. Other schools offering internships or team projects at sites outside the United States include the Wharton School and Babson College.

Utilization of Information Technology

Improvements in information and communication technologies have transformed marketing practices in recent years (for a survey, see Buzzell and Sisodia 1995). The same technologies are also being widely utilized in marketing education.

Student use of laptop computers for word processing, spreadsheet analysis, and preparation of presentations, rare in the mid-1980s, had become virtually universal by the mid-1990s. Both students and faculty at most schools also have access to various electronic databases for research purposes, including published materials from most journals and news media. Another innovation adopted by many graduate business programs is the use of networks to link students, faculty, and administrative offices. Often these networks are implemented via the Internet.

Many M.B.A. courses now provide "home pages" on the Internet, through which students can access readings and copies of presentation materials. In some cases these linkages enable students to communicate with their peers at other schools.

Other applications of information technology include multimedia case studies and the use of "groupware" by student groups to carry out group projects. Both of these were still in early stages of development in the mid-1990s.

Perhaps the ultimate use of information technology in management education is in so-called "distance learning." In a distance learning program, students rarely, if ever, come to a classroom. Instead they view videotaped lectures and participate in discussions via computer networks, all without leaving their homes or offices. Many business schools were experimenting with various forms of distance learning in the mid-1990s, most often as a way of delivering short executive education programs to companies or other groups (Byrne 1995).

A few schools have begun experimenting with M.B.A. courses delivered via distance learning media. Colorado State University, for example, was reported to offer a program in which "any qualified person in North America can receive an M.B.A. . . . without setting foot on campus" (Lord 1995, p. 92) by viewing class sessions that have been videotaped in regular on-campus meetings. The University of Michigan has offered M.B.A. courses via video links with companies in Korea and Hong Kong. Another vehicle for distance learning in the management field is a program established by Westcott Communications in partnership with several business schools including the Wharton School and Babson College (Byrne 1995).

Other Program Innovations

While some business schools have developed graduate programs specializing in international management, others have differentiated their products by specializing in particular industries or occupations.

Recent examples include health care management, entrepreneurial management (Callan and Warshaw 1994), and management in high tech industries. Within marketing, various schools offer specialized courses in these areas and in the marketing of financial services and consulting services (the latter at the Wharton School). It should be noted, however, that merely offering a single specialized course in marketing for a particular industry does not necessarily imply any long-term commitment by a school to the field. Indeed, such specialized courses often reflect transitory faculty interests rather than any enduring response to a market need.

The trend toward greater industry specialization is, in a way, a reversion to a model used in the earliest days of management education. In the early 20th century, before there were textbooks or scholarly journals in such fields as marketing, the pioneer business schools made extensive use of visiting, part-time, or retired executives to teach courses on the management of specific industries such as banking and transportation.

The increasing number of custom-designed programs developed for individual corporate clients by business schools also reflects this trend toward increasing industry specialization in M.B.A. programs. Usually these are short nondegree programs; many deal with marketing subjects.

Another program innovation that was widely adopted in the 1980s and 1990s is the executive M.B.A. (E.M.B.A.) program. This is a part-time program in which the students attend classes on a resident basis for only several weeks at the beginning and again at the end of the program. Between residency periods, classes are held all day on alternating Fridays and Saturdays, so that the time is only partly taken away from the students' jobs. Most E.M.B.A. programs include an overseas study tour of one or two weeks' duration.

E.M.B.A. programs were offered by some 120 American and foreign schools in 1995 (Kantor 1995). More than two-thirds of these programs have been introduced since 1980.

Prospects for the Future

In this section we suggest some likely directions for change in marketing education in the years ahead. Some of the changes will affect almost all educational institutions and programs in similar ways; others will have varying impacts. A greater emphasis on specialized programs designed for specific industries, for example, may be an unattractive prospect for some schools but a significant opportunity for others.

The future prospects for business schools can be considered in terms of "scenarios." To illustrate a range of possibilities, three such scenarios are presented below.

Scenario 1: Business (Schools) as Usual

In this scenario, university-based business schools continue to dominate undergraduate and graduate business education, and operate in much the same ways as before.

Supporting evidence: Traditional programs are still doing well; after a dip during the recession years 1990-92, applications to leading M.B.A. programs have increased. Many schools have modified their programs in response to the criticisms noted earlier in this paper.

We believe that the weight of the evidence suggests that this scenario is unlikely. A sense of urgency for change and renewal has affected many, if not most, business schools in recent years. As a result, they have initiated significant improvement efforts, and others will undoubtedly follow suit. The momentum for change that has been created would be very difficult to stop or reverse at this point.

A second factor is that pressures resulting from changing demographic patterns will make "business as usual" impractical. The number of students enrolled in university-based graduate management education programs in the United States will increase only slightly, and may well decline, between 1995 and 2015. This prediction is based on these figures:

> ➤ The number of men and women in the age groups from which applicants for M.B.A. programs are drawn will not increase. For example, according to the Census Bureau's "middle series" projections, the number of men and women aged 25-34 will decline steadily from 41.7 million in 1995 to 36.8 million in 2005 (U.S. Bureau of the Census 1994).

> ➤ The rate of labor force participation by women, which increased sharply in the 1970s and 1980s, has leveled off and is unlikely to increase further in the next two decades.

> ➤ The proportion of men and women of college age earning undergraduate college degrees has also leveled off and will most likely remain stable.

In light of these demographic trends, we believe that marketing education cannot revert to traditional patterns.

Scenario 2: The Barbarians Storm the Gates

At the opposite extreme from scenario 1, in our second scenario business schools lose their competitive advantage. Consulting firms and other companies enter the field in a major way, as corporations increasingly choose to "make" rather than "buy." Groups of companies increasingly band together to sponsor customized courses.

Supporting evidence: The application by consulting firm Arthur D. Little for accreditation of its program by the AACSB could be the harbinger of widespread entry by consultants. The expansion by the Keller Graduate School into 18 metropolitan markets during the 1990s is another form of non-university-based competition.

We do not believe that competition from non-university-based management education programs will have a major impact, for the following reasons:

➤ While Arthur D. Little has made a very visible move into the area of business education, we believe they are the exception rather than the rule. We view it as highly unlikely that many major consulting firms will ever venture into the business school "business," primarily because the return on this use of their staff resources is not as great as the return for time billed to client projects. It would also be difficult for consulting firm staff members to maintain the degree of objectivity that is needed for effective teaching.

➤ Likewise, the possibility that corporations will move toward in-house education on a large scale is also small, in our opinion. The in-house trend runs counter to the more widespread trend toward outsourcing of ancillary functions to outside specialists.

➤ Many schools are paying increased attention to more formalized training for faculty members in instructional design and delivery techniques, an area largely neglected in the past. Business schools must improve their capabilities in pedagogy. By being first to deploy cutting-edge instructional methodologies and technologies, they can substantially blunt the edge of new competitors. This more "scientific" orientation to teaching will, we believe, result in better teaching quality across the board; while it may not create "star" teachers, it will raise the average performance considerably.

➤ Through continuous and creative adaptation, business schools can continue to be relevant and vital institutions. If schools leverage their core competencies in the areas of knowledge creation and rigorous assessment of industry practices, they will fulfill a role that no other institution can do as well.

Scenario 3: Rejuvenating a Mature Industry

In our third scenario, significant consolidation occurs within the "industry." A handful of large, "brand name" schools dominate, extending their reach nationally and globally through greater use of information and communications technologies. Most smaller or stand-alone schools become affiliated with national players as franchisees. A number of schools establish viable niches as specialists in particular areas and parlay those into high levels of visibility.

Supporting evidence: Evidence supporting scenario 3 includes recent increases in the number of joint ventures between schools. In addition, the number of specialized programs targeted at specific industries has grown steadily. In light of these trends, we believe that scenario 3 is the most likely for the years ahead. Principally, we see four key drivers that will lead to a reshaping of this maturing industry:

> *Technology:* Information and communications technologies will allow schools to increase efficiency by increasing their reach and lowering costs.

> *Markets:* Business schools will expand the scope of their served markets, embracing growth through globalization. Like many other industries, they will discover the lure of large emerging markets and seek rapid entry into those markets.

> *Customers:* A heightened focus on customers (students as well as potential employers) will lead schools to embrace concepts such as "mass customization" and "relationship management."

> *Competition:* Intensifying competition will lead schools to segment the market, create differentiated offerings, and position them in unique ways in the market.

While the overall demand for graduate management education in the United States will be static for the next decade or more, it seems likely that demand for specialized programs and customized short educational programs will continue to grow. As a result, conventional "general-purpose" M.B.A. programs will represent a declining share of some business schools' product lines. For the leading business schools, specialized and customized programs will remain a profitable sideline to their general-purpose M.B.A. programs. For schools that lack the reputations and resources of the leaders, specialization may be the only viable route to survival in the years ahead.

With schools competing to maintain or increase their shares of a static market for management education, we expect to see increases in their advertising and sales promotion efforts, both to attract applicants for admission and to stimulate demand for graduates. Also, promotional claims will become more explicitly comparative, following the pattern typical of competition in mature industries.

M.B.A. Curriculum and Instruction

As noted earlier, many business schools began making significant revisions in their M.B.A. curricula during the late 1980s and early 1990s. At the same time, advances in information and communication technology spurred changes in instructional methods.

At many schools, curriculum changes included both additional courses dealing with international aspects of management and courses or projects on the management of cross-functional business processes such as new product development and customer service. To implement these changes, business school faculty members—including those in marketing—must redirect significant amounts of their time and resources toward the development and testing of new teaching materials.

To the extent that marketing faculty members devote their energies to the development and teaching of new courses, less time and fewer resources will be available for traditional research pursuits. One consequence of this shift in faculty agendas is that schools may need to revise criteria for evaluating faculty performance. At most of the leading American business schools, faculty performance has been judged predominantly on the basis of published, peer-reviewed research work. Course design and development has been given little weight, except where it is directly related to research. This will need to change.

There will undoubtedly be major increases in the utilization of information and communication technologies in marketing education in the years ahead, some of which may require substantial resources. One very promising area for utilizing information technology, for example, is in the development of "multimedia case studies," which might include still pictures and full-motion video segments, together with data in spreadsheet form and text. Experience to date indicates that the production costs for such multimedia materials are very high. Only resource-rich business schools will be able to afford to produce this type of instructional material; other schools will have to import multimedia materials from the leading institutions, or rely on corporate sponsors to support their own development projects.

Academic Research and Development in Marketing

Pressure from practitioners for greater relevance in marketing education will strongly influence academic agendas for research and development in the years ahead. Many of the changes now underway in marketing systems and practices are not yet adequately reflected in academic research or in the content of marketing courses. These include:

> ➤ The growth of "partnership" agreements between suppliers and customers, such as the much-discussed arrangement between Procter & Gamble and Wal-Mart. Such partnerships are aimed at improving distribution channel efficiency, via reduced costs and by linking inventory replenishment directly to the sales or usage of the downstream partner (see Buzzell and Ortmeyer 1995). Research is needed to determine how partnerships can most effectively be managed.

➤ Related to the growth of buyer-seller partnerships is the growing importance of "relationship marketing." Often the relationship between a marketer and a major account is managed by a cross-functional account team that includes operations, finance, marketing, and management information systems in addition to sales. The role of sales and marketing managers in major account teams differs considerably from their traditional, more independent role as the sole or primary contact between a firm and its customers.

➤ Fueled by advances in information technology, database marketing has grown dramatically since the mid-1980s. While some new courses dealing with database marketing have been introduced, the subject has not yet received widespread attention in mainstream marketing courses.

➤ On a more conceptual level, Prahalad (1995) has pointed out that traditional research paradigms must be rethought in light of the transformations that are occurring in many global industries. He suggests, for example, that a business unit's share of a finished product market (such as VCRs) may no longer be a valid measure of its "market influence." One reason is that the unit's end-product market share may differ substantially from its share of manufacturing output, its share of "core product" output, and its underlying relative strength in the "competencies" required for effective competition. Academic research might be directed, first, to developing empirical data based on alternative measures of market influence and, then, to exploring relationships between market influence and business performance.

These and other changes in marketing practice are discussed in greater detail elsewhere in this volume.

Research-Teaching Linkages

The relative importance of teaching and research has long been a controversial issue in business schools. In part, this debate reflects an implicit zero-sum or "trade-off"-oriented view of these two primary components of professorial responsibility. We believe that a more symbiotic and synergistic relationship will emerge between teaching and research in the future. As a result, the reward system will no longer make distinctions or trade-offs between superior teaching and research; rather, schools will demand, and receive, integrated excellence in both arenas.

Related is the issue of how much universities are pressured to conduct "applied" research with readily apparent impact on business practice. Most schools will no longer have the luxury of supporting relatively unconstrained research agendas.

Pragmatic, applied research will, almost by definition, have greater and more immediate practical and economic value in the marketplace. As a result, we anticipate an escalating emphasis on better dissemination and more concerted, focused efforts to directly influence practice. Individual faculty members and/or business schools will make greater efforts to create commercial products and programs based on their research.

We project the following trends to continue:

➤ Greater and more formalized linkages between teaching and research agendas. Faculty will be given incentives to align their research agendas with current business concerns, publish in both academic and managerially oriented journals, and develop related M.B.A.-level and executive courses.

➤ A movement from *ad hoc* to formalized and focused research activity at the institutional level. Research agendas will be related to the distinctive positioning plank adopted by the school—something that, in a mature market, we believe the majority of schools will be forced to do. Thus, in 1995 Emory University's marketing department hired faculty with the explicit understanding that their research agendas include a strong focus on relationship marketing. Likewise, Vanderbilt University emphasizes services marketing and the impact of the Internet on marketing.

➤ The establishment of more corporate-supported research and executive education centers at business schools (examples include the Center for Relationship Marketing at Emory's Goizueta Business School and the FedEx-supported Center for Cycle Time Research at Memphis).

➤ A greater degree of exchange of faculty and corporate resources. Senior executives may increasingly take sabbaticals at business schools, while faculty will be encouraged to spend time at corporations in line functions.

Other Issues

In recent years, as applications for M.B.A. programs declined and tuition levels rose, leading schools became highly competitive in their efforts to attract students. Some observers believe that the need to fill classes led to a dilution of student quality. Others believe that many current students have little experience with negative feedback, a weak team ethic (they are told repeatedly that they are special), a short attention span, and a high expectation to be entertained. Critics also contend that there is an increased level of "pandering" to students, who are now referred to at many schools as "customers."

How will this play out in the future? The first problem may be a cyclical one; in 1994 and 1995, applications to leading schools have risen significantly. This will likely alleviate some of the pressures that have led schools to entertain and pander. We believe that discerning students (as most will be) will be drawn to more demanding programs and to the more demanding courses within those programs. Programs that do not "stretch" students in a significant way will suffer in reputation.

With regard to whether students will be or should be treated as "customers," there is no clear answer. At many schools, especially those not in the top tier, the primary customer appears to be the business community that hires the graduates of the program. Students are viewed as either the "product," to which value is added during the M.B.A. program, or as "partners" in the educational process. The latter metaphor can also be reasonably applied to hiring companies. Clearly, there is a complex web of relationships between business schools and companies; in addition to being customers and partners, companies are also suppliers (of part-time students and adjunct faculty) and potential competitors.

Another trend currently affecting management education is the increasing number of students going into finance, investment banking, consulting, and other staff positions. To critics, this reflects a mistaken belief that operational aspects of business (such as operations and marketing) do not matter. We believe this is a cyclical phenomenon; in the late 1980s, there was a distinct shift in U.S. M.B.A. programs into marketing and manufacturing, as these had been identified as areas where U.S. companies lagged behind their global competitors. With the U.S. resurgence in competitiveness, and the bull market of recent years, interest in these operating areas has once again ebbed. One would hope for a less cyclical pattern over time; however, business schools, above all, are market-driven entities.

A major opportunity in the future will be the need to "re-train" M.B.A.s who have been out for, say, 20 years or more. The "lifelong learning" model will become increasingly popular in business education. Students may return to their alma mater or go elsewhere for condensed M.B.A. refresher courses. While few schools have specifically targeted this niche, we believe it will become an important one. It reflects a long-term relationship orientation between schools and students that appears to be very timely.

Conclusion

Ever since marketing courses were first offered in the early 20th century, academics have faced the challenge of keeping pace with the "real world" of marketing institutions and practices. The changes that are taking place in the 1990s are creating new needs for research and course development that will continue as the field of marketing enters its second century. For marketing education to respond to these changes effectively, close cooperation between business schools and practitioners will be essential. The Marketing Science Institute has played a major role in fostering such cooperation for almost four decades; we are confident that it will continue to do so in the 21st century. ■

➤ 6

Some Thoughts on the Futures of Marketing

Donald R. Lehmann

What We Have (and Haven't) Done

Having smart people speculate about the future is always both instructive and frustrating. Hopefully this volume has been instructive in several ways. I am extremely grateful to the authors for taking the time to participate in this effort.

Steve Greyser's piece nicely ties the current situation to the past. While I will resist the temptation to quote a well-known French proverb, it is clear that we have much to learn from the past. In fact, two major, related trends—benchmarking (best-practice studies) and the development of empirical generalizations—are essentially histori-cal analyses done under the implicit assumption that things will work in the future as they have in the past. Studying history is both com-forting and productive since, in general, change is evolutionary and even cyclical. Fundamental principles recur, in spite of our tendency to invent new/contemporary jargon to describe them. Customers will continue to matter and consequently operating businesses will contin-ue to strive to serve their needs—the essence of marketing. Further, improvements in information technology and communication make long-term customer relations even more crucial in the future.

The rosy picture for the marketing concept, however, will not necessarily transfer to the marketing function/department. Fred Webster and George Day separately and eloquently discuss the coming order. In their new if not brave world, the core of marketing continues its evolution from transportation and distribution through sales, the marketing mix (4Ps), and strategy to general procedures (aka processes) linking the company to the customer. Supply chains, product development, database marketing, and concepts such as brand and customer equity are supplanting the 4Ps and traditional measures of success such as sales and share as marketing's critical activities and concerns. Given that these processes are inherently interfunctional, marketing's position vis-à-vis operations, design, R&D, sales, etc. is unclear. Sadly the current evidence suggests a gradual erosion of the marketing department as the "lead partner" in these efforts.

Possibly the most poignant (at least to a professor) scenario is the future role of marketing within business schools. As the paper by Bob Buzzell and Raj Sisodia suggests, academic institutions are resistant to fundamental change (though certainly not fads), especially when they require interdepartmental cooperation. The result is a competition among areas, with finance winning, management and potentially operations holding their own (partly by annexing topics previously addressed by marketing such as strategy, product development, and customer service), and marketing slipping. Schools increasingly have a prestige order (at least in terms of M.B.A.s' job preferences) of (1) investment banking, (2) consulting, and (3) other. The resulting lack of enthusiasm for marketing is both apparent and inappropriate. Financial markets are after all markets, with customers whose preferences (either innate or created) are studied and whose needs are serviced with various financial instruments (e.g., derivatives, mutual funds) through direct sales, direct marketing, etc. Consulting jobs often focus on selecting markets to serve and developing processes to create new products or efficiently and effectively interface with customers. Put bluntly, the core of finance and consulting is customer relations. Still the prestige of marketing as a function has decreased, in no small measure because we have focused on ever more narrow topics and marginal improvements.

In a different look at the future, John Farley has described how the nature of the world is changing. Importantly, he also notes that many changes are gradual and predictable. For a number of reasons, our reactions to these changes often resemble that of the oft-described frog in the pot of water who tolerates the gradually increasing temperature until he boils.

In terms of changes, the impact of information technology is clearly a major development. The evolution from an agricultural economy to an industrial one, and now to a service-based one with information and computing at its core, represents a massive change. Why, then, have we not devoted more space in this volume to that topic? Basically, the answer has three parts. First, precisely because the subject is so widely discussed, it is not clear what we have to add to the deluge of stories (many a bit fanciful) already available. Second, MSI recently completed a major effort in this direction, resulting in the 1994 book edited by Bob Blattberg, Rashi Glazer, and John Little called *The Marketing Information Revolution* (see Figure 1 for the table of contents). Finally, in addition to having been widely covered both outside and inside MSI (where use of information technology remains a top research priority), the topic implicitly or explicitly is addressed in all of the chapters in this volume. As a consequence, we decided not to have a single chapter on the topic, in no small measure because no one seemed able to write one of which they were proud.

Some Personal Observations

The Task of Marketing

Marketing has changed from a preoccupation with tactics (the 4Ps) to a heavy emphasis on strategy. The recent trend suggests a new, emerging focus on a few core activities. One view of marketing is the linking of the firm through customers to long-run profits (Figure 2). As such, marketing strategy consists mainly of programs/processes such as integrated communication, product development, information

Figure 1. The Marketing Information Revolution: Table of Contents

1. Marketing in the Information Revolution

2. Point-of-Sale Data in Consumer Goods Marketing: Transforming the Art of Marketing into the Science of Marketing

3. Consumer Transaction Databases: Present Status and Prospects

4. The Evolution of Decision Support Systems and Databases in Consumer Goods Marketing

5. Expert Systems for Scanner Data in Practice

6. Generating, Managing, and Communicating Insights

7. Modeling Market Response in Large Customer Panels

8. Large-Scale Databases: The New Marketing Challenge

9. Artificial Intelligence for Designing Marketing Decision-Making Tools

10. Marketing Decision Support Systems in Transition

11. Experts and Models in Combination

12. Harnessing the Marketing Information Revolution: Toward the Market-Driven Learning Organization

13. Identifying the Legal and Ethical Risks and Costs of Using New Information Technologies to Support Marketing Programs

14. Marketing Information Technologies in Japan

15. Managing the Information-Intensive Firm of 2001

(Blattberg, Glazer, and Little 1994)

management, value and supply chain management, customer contact personnel selection and training (aka human resources), and pricing and promotion. These programs and their manifestations as the 4Ps then impact three key, related aspects of the market: (1) customer value, (2) brand equity, and (3) employee loyalty which are (the) key drivers of long-run profits.

Note the eventual goal—long-run "profits" (however defined)—has not changed. What has changed, however, is how we work to achieve them. Initial trial-and-error manipulation of price, advertising, etc. has given way to a systematic approach driven by strategy. What

Figure 2. The Marketing Concept Revisited

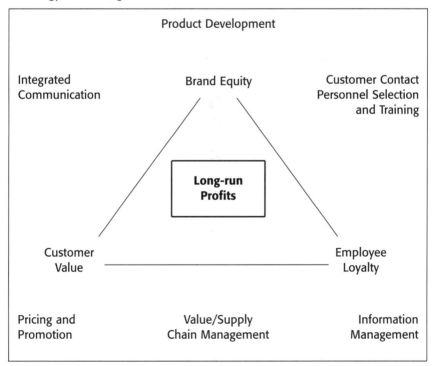

Strategy/Positioning

now seems to be occurring is the development of three, interrelated instrumental goals that are thought to mediate the impact of programs on profits, exemplified by the customer satisfaction movement. These goals relate to the attachments of customers and employees to a company (manufacturer or retailer) and the direct appeal of a company's trademark to customers (brand equity). The development of positions such as brand equity managers and the obvious link among brand, customer, and employee attitudes and loyalties suggests these measurable goals are the appropriate barometers of marketing strategy and tactics.

The Content of Marketing Courses

The implications of these shifts for marketing education are considerable. As marketing has moved from the descriptive 4Ps stage through strategy to its emerging focus on instrumental goals and processes, the core course must undergo a similar evolution. In essence, the new course blends a focus on intermediate goals and processes with the general "direct (interactive) marketingization" of marketing which has turned a little-respected offshoot known as direct mail into the driving model of much current thinking. Figure 3 provides one projection of what the future MBA marketing core course (and by implication, the function of marketing) will look like.

The Crucial Role of Research and Information in Marketing Practice

In the past, the model for research has been the special (customized) study, epitomized by a customer survey. In the future, the model will be the use of specialized existing databases (e.g., scanner panels and customer records) combined with the results of similar analyses in the past (aka empirical generalization or meta-analysis). Hence research will rely on and contribute to institutional knowledge (i.e., creating a learning organization) at least as much as it collects data about and provides guidance to specific decisions.

Downsizing has severely curtailed companies' already limited reserves devoted to knowledge development and dissemination. (Not

Figure 3. Content of the Core Marketing Course (Percent Effort By Topic)

	1950-1970	1970-1990	2005?
Marketing Concept/Philosophy	5	10	5
General Strategy	5	20	5
4Ps	80	40	20
Service	0	5	10

Instrumental Goals
  Brand Equity
  Satisfaction
  Customer Value
  Market Orientation
  Employee Loyalty
	0	5	20

Processes
  New Products
  Information Use/Research
  Customer Management/Direct Marketing
    (Acquisition, Retention, Expansion, Deletion)
  Value/Supply Chain Management
	10	20	40

many firms have increased their research staffs or budgets even if they proclaim they are in the information age.) The resulting heavy use of consultants in effect has increased the use of "knowledge bases." In essence consultants draw on experience in one venue to suggest actions in another, albeit typically in a qualitative way. Hence using consultants produces results that are largely influenced by the analogous situations on which they draw.

The evolution to analysis of existing data began with the growth of syndicated services (e.g., Simmons), diary panels (e.g., MRCA), and government data. Here a trade-off emerged between specificity/relevance and timeliness/cost, with specialized surveys still preferred in the majority of cases. The balance shifted further toward the use of existing data with the development of scanner panels and their use first by manufacturers and then by retailers. Finally, the development of extensive customer records data has made analysis of existing data the key research activity. Hence we have gone from reliance on special studies with syndicated data playing an ancillary role to reliance on existing data with occasional use of special studies to augment available information.

In the 1960s, a manager in paper towels would routinely sneer at the notion that someone who had worked on soap or even toilet tissue or paper napkins knew anything of relevance. ("They just don't understand our business.") A major break in mindset occurred with the acceptance of benchmarking as a tool for improvement. Whatever its merits (and small, unrepresentative-sample-based qualitative methods have plenty of weaknesses), it legitimized the notion that a manager could learn something from someone in a different business. In the 1990s, spurred on by the twin forces of global competition and downsizing (however renamed), managers are forced to look beyond their industry, as it was once defined, for both threats and opportunities as well as ways to improve. Given the increased pressure to justify expenditures quantitatively (as opposed to by rhetoric/faith alone), managers now tend to seek out specific answers to difficult questions.

Particularly interesting in this process has been a flip-flop in positions between managers and academics. Whereas in the past academics carried the banner for generalizations and quantitative results, currently managers seem at least as interested in them as most academics (many of whom are moving in the direction of in-depth case studies). In fact, in the 1993-95 MSI priorities ballot, managers rated empirical generalizations as higher in priority than did academics.

To be more explicit, the role of empirical generalizations will increase in importance at the expense of creativity/decision freedom. Like it or not, most of what we do has parallels in the past and it would be pretty stupid to condemn ourselves to repeat old mistakes. Hence for many situations, we will begin with a model of impacts (e.g., advertising dollars on sales) based on past studies and information and adjust it based on current information/intuition (rather than vice versa as we have done in the past). In the extreme, research will consist of Bayesian-type combinations of past results and current data augmented by focus groups and direct customer-contact-based intuition.

Data mining is an accepted if controversial and increasingly powerful technique. Neural nets and similar procedures scan data looking for patterns and are hence the next generation of stepwise procedures such as AID and CHAID. Since, like their predecessors, they rely on higher-order interactions and often overfit data, they are useful exploratory devices but are not well suited to producing general results. Hence such procedures will play a useful but far from fundamental role in providing parsimonious and empirically supported quantitative models of the impact of marketing variables.

More useful are formal meta-analytic procedures (see, for example, the Farley and Lehmann 1986 book published with the help of MSI). Although limited by, among other things, the representativeness of available studies, the basic purpose of generalizing across studies makes meta-analysis an obvious tool for use in marketing. Its use is likely to increase, as it already has in medicine where the life-or-death consequences of decisions have speeded its (controversial) acceptance.

Managerial Interpretation of Information

Humans are terribly inaccurate in their interpretation of information. Numerous consistent judgment biases have been found, including availability (using information that is readily available in memory or proximity), anchoring on an initial view and inadequately adjusting as more information comes in (aka researcher bias) or conversely ignoring base information and being overly influenced by specific (case) information, and overconfidence (inadequately recognizing the uncertainty in a situation). Well summarized in books by Bazerman (1994) and Russo and Schoemaker (1990), these biases influence decisions in many ways.

The biases can be dealt with in at least two ways. First, one could try to train managers to recognize and overcome these biases. It is fairly easy to get people to recognize that the biases exist, though it is not easy to get them to overcome them. Hence the second approach is to present information in such a way that the biases are canceled out or at least minimized. This has major implications for the design and use of information systems. It also raises a dilemma: should we provide accurate information we know is likely to be interpreted inaccurately or present inaccurate information which will lead to correct inferences?

Man vs. Machine in an Information Deluge

An interesting issue for the future is how much analysis and subsequently which decisions can be automated. Both the concept of decision support systems popularized by John Little, Len Lodish, etc. and the work of John McCann on his "marketing workbench" point toward computer-based systems not only for analyzing information but for drawing conclusions and making decisions as well. We are at a point where, at least for some cases, it is not clear what the manager adds to the analysis.

The increasing rate of information (or at least data) availability means one is essentially required to automate some data collection and interpretation. If I run a small store (or large business) which has 20 customers a day, I can retain significant customer information in my head. If on the other hand I run Wal-Mart, I have no choice but to automate information collection and interpretation (i.e., re-ordering decisions).

A related issue is how quickly/frequently one should respond to information. Humans tend to overcorrect/oversteer. Hence withholding information may improve decisions. Further, evidence suggests expert systems based on a manager's past decisions often outperform the manager in future decisions. Taken together this suggests that at least for tactical, repetitive decisions, it will be beneficial to automate responses and give the manager a limited number of opportunities to intervene or overrule the system.

The Internet

The Internet is obviously a major "event," and its impacts are widespread. Taking a more historical and less hysterical view, however, it can be viewed as "just another" communication improvement, following language, the printing press, newspapers, mail, telegraph, telephone, TV, and fax, and to some extent the automobile. It is not clear that on theoretical grounds it is more radical or really new. Indeed, it has been around in some form for at least 25 years so a generation has come and gone without its having much impact. Moreover it is currently limited to two of the five senses (sight, sound) that are covered by previous communication methods.

What is clear is that the Internet has major implications for communication on three dimensions: speed, scope, and (at least currently) cost. With respect to speed, information diffusion is clearly much faster than before. While in earlier eras discussions of the merits of products (and political candidates) required weeks through letters to the editor and editorials/stories, consumer/public reaction is now essentially instantaneous. This raises some interesting research issues:

1. Measuring the development and impact of "Word of Web"

2. Assessing the opportunities for and impacts of foul play on the Web including misleading information, fake input to interest groups, and false hits on sites that impact their subsequent attractiveness (Hansen 1996)

3. Addressing legal remedies

With respect to scope, the Internet is essentially international (knows no borders) and may well encourage more global branding and product design. On the other hand, large portions of the developing world (and the majority of the United States as well) are not on the Web, so concentrating all efforts on the Web is clearly myopic.

Some general issues raised by the development of the Internet include:

1. What will be the role of traditional publishing of both research journals and textbooks as well as general circulation magazines and books? Since publishers subcontract design, typesetting, production, etc., do they have any role (other than delaying the availability of information) in the information value chain?

2. What will be the relation of this channel to both full-service retailers (department, specialty stores) and discounters?

3. What will the Internet's impact be on the general sociology of the family and the community? Will we develop "keyboard potatoes" who are essentially asocial beings?

Most important, if we are to develop a meaningful interpretation of the Internet's current and future impact, research in this area must focus on the constructs underlying the Web (speed, etc.) and not just the medium itself.

New Horizons

Marketing is not limited to large companies in the industrial northern hemisphere. Whole continents (e.g., South America) are largely ignored by many researchers, businesses, and even financial markets, as are small businesses (which are responsible for the majority of job and wealth creation). While it seems likely that most of what we know transfers, it is strange that we spend almost no time researching or even thinking about these other areas. Different cultural attitudes and resource bases have implications for everything from negotiating tactics and ad copy to concepts of brand and customer loyalty. We would benefit from extending our sights a bit in these directions.

The Value of Marketing

In an era where financial analysts drive markets, it is crucial to justify activities in ways that managers and their publics understand. This means general statements such as "we're building for the future" and concepts such as "customer franchise building" are inadequate justifications for expenditures. We simply must generate measures that are (a) sound and (b) clearly and quantifiably related to financial performance (stock price) or its immediate determinants (sales, profits). Measures like awareness and attitude just won't do. Rather we must relate marketing actions either directly to sales and profits (or price/margins) or to things that indisputably lead to them. Hence franchise-building activities (e.g., advertising) must focus on (a) brand equity or (b) the value of customers. (Even satisfaction tends to operate through the loyalty component of brand equity and through the future volume of business aspect of the value of a customer.) Here again, cumulated evidence from past results should help bolster the case for these impacts as well as sharpen our estimates of them.

In addition to proving the business worth of marketing, it is important to demonstrate both its responsible practice and a positive (or at least neutral) impact on societal welfare. Not only an issue in various countries around the world, antimarketing sentiment is widespread and influential in the United States as well. Both products themselves and marketing methods (including the use of customer data which is transforming how we practice marketing) are under intense scrutiny. Every four years in the United States the race for the presidency brings new (and largely justified) condemnation of the "packaging" process. Perhaps we should at least point out that what is going on in political campaigns is more sales than marketing.

While marketers cannot "win" in many of these discussions, being perceived as a biased/interested party, their absence from the debate is bothersome. As Professor Thomas Kinnear, among others, has commented, why is it that when questions of consumer welfare arise lawyers' and economists' opinions are solicited and ours are not?

Of course social issues put one squarely in the domain of ethics, an arena in which most of us are uncomfortable. There are no easy answers but the failure to address at least some of the issues is a clear ethical statement as well. Hopefully our future in this area will be a bit more glorious than our past.

Whither Marketing?

If, as Regis McKenna suggests, "marketing is everything" (1991), it is also nothing. Focus on customers is now at least discussed by people in R&D, design, quality departments, operations, and even finance. While this is potentially very good for business, it is not good for the marketing function per se. Further, if responsibility becomes too divided it may not be exercised at all and the marketing credo will become like many mission statements, words often mouthed but rarely implemented.

In order to sharpen the issue, consider two future scenarios. In one future, marketing's roles include:

1. Being an important/"lead" partner in

    ➤ Making long-run strategic decisions such as what business or region to be in

    ➤ Developing, testing, and introducing new products

2. Acting as the guardian of the marketing philosophy/vision that places satisfied customers at the core of operating business

3. Providing the central focus of learning/information about the external environment

4. Being in charge of customer

    ➤ Acquisition

    ➤ Retention (loyalty)

    ➤ Expansion (cross-selling)

> ➤ Deletion (euthanasia)

5. Being responsible for monitoring and improving interrelated instrumental goals such as

   > ➤ Brand equity

   > ➤ Satisfaction

   > ➤ Value of customers

   > ➤ Market orientation

6. Being responsible for the 4Ps, plus service, for existing products

7. Providing input to public policy decisions regarding such marketing issues as product design and advertising as well as input into broader debates about the impact of marketing on an economy and a society

In another, less appealing scenario, marketing loses control over six of these areas and becomes solely an implementer of the 4Ps (sans service)—essentially the department of cents-off coupons and blue-light specials. It appears we may be moving in this direction. In the words of Melville's Bartleby the Scrivener, "I prefer not."

Summary

Undoubtedly these essays have left you a bit unsatisfied. After all we haven't produced a single scenario or detailed forecast, partly since this would be misleadingly precise. Neither have we presented an entirely rosy outlook for the field. In our defense, we didn't try to. Rather we attempted to provide some thoughts and stimulate others. If two or three concepts presented here had an impact on you, we consider the endeavor a success. Stay tuned for future ruminations about the future, including a special issue of the *Journal of Marketing* edited by George Day and Dave Montgomery targeted for 1999, just in time for the next millennium. ∎

About the Contributors

Robert D. Buzzell is Distinguished Professor of Marketing at the School of Business Administration, George Mason University. He is also Sebastian S. Kresge Professor of Business Administration, Emeritus, at the Harvard Business School. In 1967, he was visiting professor at the European Institute of Business Administration (INSEAD). He received his Ph.D. from Ohio State University, M.S. from the University of Illinois, and A.B. from George Washington University. Professor Buzzell is the author or coauthor of numerous books and articles. From 1968-72 he served as MSI's Executive Director, and played a major role in the PIMS (Profit Impact of Market Strategies) program.

George S. Day is the Geoffrey T. Boisi Professor and Director of the Huntsman Center for Global Competition and Innovation at the Wharton School at the University of Pennsylvania. He received his Ph.D. from Columbia University. With research interests in managing new product development, strategic planning, and competitive strategies in global markets, he has written 12 books and over 100 articles for marketing and management journals. He is the recipient of various awards, including the Charles Coolidge Parlin Award in 1994 and the Paul D. Converse Award in 1996. Professor Day served as MSI's Executive Director from 1989-91.

John U. Farley is the C. V. Starr Distinguished Research Fellow at the Amos Tuck School of Business Administration, Dartmouth College, and the Henkel Professor of Industrial Marketing at the China Europe International Business School in Shanghai. He received his B.A. and M.B.A. degrees from Dartmouth College and

Ph.D. from the University of Chicago, and was on the faculty of Carnegie-Mellon University, the Wharton School at the University of Pennsylvania, and Columbia University. With research interests in marketing strategy in world markets, the development and application of management science techniques to problems in marketing, and forecasting and marketing information system development, Professor Farley has published in numerous journals, and has coauthored several books including *Meta-Analysis in Marketing* (with Donald Lehmann). He served as MSI's Executive Director from 1985-87.

Stephen A. Greyser is the Richard P. Chapman Professor of Business Administration at the Harvard Business School, where he specializes in consumer marketing, advertising, and corporate communications. A graduate of Harvard College, he received M.B.A. and D.B.A. degrees from Harvard Business School, where he was the Chirurg Advertising Fellow. He is responsible for 12 books, is a frequent contributor to journals on marketing, advertising, and business/consumer attitudes, and has published some 250 case studies. His current research areas include corporate communications, corporate reputation, marketing-advertising and public policy, and the business of sports. He is also a director or trustee of several corporate and nonprofit organizations. Professor Greyser served as MSI's Executive Director from 1972-81, and subsequently as a long-time Trustee.

Stephan H. Haeckel is Director of Strategic Studies at IBM's Advanced Business Institute, where his area of concentration is the strategic impact of information and information technology. His current focus is a business model for organizations that must cope in environments of unpredictable change, called the "Sense and Respond" model. He has also served as director of Advanced Market Development for IBM, and was one of the authors of IBM's corporate services strategy. Mr. Haeckel has been published by the Harvard Business School Press, and the *Harvard Business Review*, as well as MSI. He received engineering and M.B.A. degrees from Washington University. Mr. Haeckel is Chairman of MSI's Executive Committee.

Donald R. Lehmann is George E. Warren Professor of Business at the Columbia University Graduate School of Business. He has a B.S. degree in mathematics from Union College, Schenectady, New York, and an M.S.I.A. and Ph.D. from the Krannert School, Purdue University. His research interests include modeling individual choice and decision making, understanding group and interdependent decisions, meta-analysis, and the introduction and adoption of innovations. He has taught courses in marketing, management, and statistics at Columbia, and has also taught at Cornell, Dartmouth, and New York University. He has authored a number of journal articles and books, and was founding editor of *Marketing Letters*. Professor Lehmann served as MSI's Executive Director from 1993-95 and as President of the Association for Consumer Research in 1995.

Rajendra Sisodia is Associate Professor of Marketing at George Mason University. Previously he was Assistant Professor of Marketing at Boston University. Professor Sisodia has a bachelor's degree in electrical and electronics engineering from the Birla Institute of Technology and Science, in Pilani, India, and an M.B.A. from the Bajaj Institute of Management Studies, Bombay. He has an M.Phil. and Ph.D. in marketing and business policy from Columbia University. His research interests include marketing productivity, strategic uses of information technology in business, database marketing, and quantitative methods in marketing. Professor Sisodia has published over 40 articles in conference proceedings and journals, and coauthored *The Consolidation of the Information Industry*, published in 1996.

Frederick E. Webster, Jr., is the Charles Henry Jones Third Century Professor of Management at the Amos Tuck School of Business Administration, Dartmouth College, where he has been on the faculty since 1965. He earned his Ph.D. at Stanford University's Graduate School of Business and was on the faculty at the Graduate School of Business at Columbia University, before returning to Dartmouth where he had earned his bachelor's and master's degrees. Professor Webster has also been a visiting professor at the International Management Institute in Geneva, Switzerland. His research in marketing strategy, industrial marketing, salesforce management, corporate culture, and buyer behavior has resulted in over 50 journal articles and book chapters, and a dozen books. He served as MSI's Executive Director from 1987-89. ■

About MSI

MSI was established in 1961 as a not-for-profit institute with the goal of bringing together business leaders and academics to create knowledge that will improve business performance. The primary mission was to provide intellectual leadership in marketing and its allied fields.

Over the years, MSI's global network of scholars from leading graduate schools of management and thought leaders from sponsoring corporations has expanded to encompass multiple business functions and disciplines.

Issues of key importance to business performance are identified by the Board of Trustees, which represents MSI corporations and the academic community. MSI supports studies by academics on these issues and disseminates the results through conferences and workshops, as well as through its publications series. ■

References

AACSB (American Assembly of Collegiate Schools of Business) (1978), *Policies, Procedures, and Standards*. St. Louis: AACSB.

_____ (1980), *Policies, Procedures, and Standards*. St. Louis: AACSB.

_____ (1995), "MBA Program Changes Prove Value Does Not Come Cheaply." *Newsline* 36 (Fall), 1-6.

Ansoff, H. Igor (1965), *Corporate Strategy: An Analytic Approach to Business Policy for Growth and Expansion*. New York: McGraw-Hill.

Arthur D. Little, Inc. (1996), "Master of Science in Management Program 1996-1997." Cambridge, MA: Arthur D. Little.

Bagozzi, Richard P. (1975), "Marketing as Exchange." *Journal of Marketing* 39 (4) (October), 32-9.

Baker, Michael J. (1995), "The Future of Marketing." In *Companion Encyclopedia of Marketing*, ed. Michael J. Baker. London, New York: Routledge.

Barabba, Vincent P. (1995), *Meeting of the Minds: Creating the Market-Based Enterprise*. Boston: Harvard Business School Press.

Bauer, Raymond A., and Stephen A. Greyser (1967), "The Dialogue That Never Happens." *Harvard Business Review* 45 (6) (November-December), 2-12, 186-90.

Bazerman, Max H. (1994), *Judgment in Managerial Decision Making*. New York: Wiley.

Beddow, Thomas F. (1995), Handouts for Panel Discussion: "Developing Future Market Leaders." Marketing Science Institute Board of Trustees Meeting, Dana Point, California, November 9-10.

Behrman, Jack N., and Richard I. Levin (1984), "Are Business Schools Doing Their Job?" *Harvard Business Review* 62 (1) (January-February), 140-7.

Blattberg, Robert C. (1995), "The Marketing Information Revolution and New Marketing Paradigms." Presentation to the Marketing Science Institute Board of Trustees Meeting, Dana Point, California, November 9-10.

Blattberg, Robert C., Rashi Glazer, and John D. C. Little, eds. (1994), *The Marketing Information Revolution*. Boston: Harvard Business School Press.

———, and Scott A. Neslin (1989), "Sales Promotion: The Long and the Short of It." *Marketing Letters* 1 (1) (December), 81-97.

Blau, Peter M. (1956), *Bureaucracy in Modern Society*. New York: Random House.

Bluestein, Abraham I. (1994), "Leadership Practices in Marketing." *Planning Review* 22 (September-October), 35-6.

Borden, Neil H. (1964), "The Concept of the Marketing Mix." *Journal of Advertising Research* (June), 2-7.

Business and Society Review (1995), "Has Business School Education Become a Scandal?" (No. 93) (Spring), 4-16.

Buzzell, Robert D., and Bradley T. Gale (1987), *The PIMS Principles: Linking Strategy to Performance*. New York: The Free Press.

Buzzell, Robert D., and Gwen Ortmeyer (1995), "Channel Partnerships Streamline Distribution." *Sloan Management Review* 36 (3) (Spring), 85-96.

Buzzell, Robert D., and Rajendra Sisodia (1995), "Information Technology and Marketing." In *Companion Encyclopedia of Marketing*, ed. Michael J. Baker, 301-17. London, New York: Routledge.

Byrne, John A. (1991), "Weekend Warriors: A Guide to MBAs for Working Execs." *Business Week* (October 28), 109-14.

Byrne, John A. (1995), "Virtual B-Schools: Beaming Classes to Companies from Daewoo to Disney." *Business Week* (October 23), 64-8.

Byrne, John A., and Lori Bongiorno (1994), "The Best B-Schools." *Business Week* (October 24), 62-70.

Callan, Katherine, and Michael Warshaw (1994), "The 25 Best Business Schools for Entrepreneurs." *Success* (September), 37-50.

Capon, Noel, John U. Farley, and Scott Hoenig (1996), *Toward an Integrative Explanation of Corporate Financial Performance.* Boston: Kluwer Academic Publishers, 1996.

Capon, Noel, John U. Farley, and James M. Hulbert (1988), *Corporate Strategic Planning.* New York: Columbia University Press.

Capon, Noel, John U. Farley, Donald R. Lehmann, and James M. Hulbert (1992), "Profiles of Product Innovators among Large U.S. Manufacturers." *Management Science* 38 (2) (February), 157-69.

Cespedes, Frank V. (1995), *Concurrent Marketing: Integrating Product, Sales and Service.* Boston: Harvard Business School Press.

Chandler, Alfred D. (1962), *Strategy and Structure: Chapters in the History of the Industrial Enterprise.* Cambridge, MA: MIT Press.

Cheit, Earl F. (1985), "Business Schools and Their Critics." *California Management Review* 27 (3) (Spring), 43-62.

Collis, David, and Pankaj Ghemawat (1994), "Industry Analysis: Understanding Industry Structure and Dynamics." In *The Portable MBA in Strategy*, eds. Liam Fahey and Robert M. Randall. New York: Wiley.

Commission on Admission to Graduate Management Education (1990), *Leadership for a Changing World: The Future Role of Graduate Management Education.* Los Angeles: Graduate Management Admissions Council.

Corey, E. Raymond, and Steven H. Star (1971), *Organization Strategy: A Marketing Approach.* Boston: Harvard University, Graduate School of Business Administration, Division of Research.

Davenport, Thomas (1993), *Process Innovation: Reengineering Work Through Information Technology.* Boston: Harvard Business School Press.

Day, George S. (1992), "Marketing's Contribution to the Strategy Dialogue." *Journal of the Academy of Marketing Science* 20 (4) (Fall), 323-30.

_____ (1994), "The Capabilities of Market-Driven Organizations." *Journal of Marketing* 58 (4) (October), 37-52.

_____ (1995), "Strategies, Capabilities, and Marketing Activities." Presentation to the Marketing Science Institute Board of Trustees Meeting, Dana Point, California, November 9-10.

Deshpandé, Rohit, John U. Farley, and Frederick E. Webster, Jr. (1993), "Corporate Culture, Customer Orientation, and Innovativeness in Japanese Firms: A Quadrad Analysis." *Journal of Marketing* 57 (1) (January), 23-37.

_____, _____, and _____ (1996), "A Five-Country Comparison of How Corporate Culture and Climate, Customer Orientation and Innovativeness Affect Performance." Hanover, NH: The Amos Tuck School, Working Paper.

Drucker, Peter F. (1954), *The Practice of Management*. New York: Harper & Row.

The Economist (1994), "Death of the Brand Manager" (April 9), 67-8.

Elliott, Clifford J., Jack S. Goodwin, and James C. Goodwin (1994), "MBA Programs and Business Needs: Is There a Mismatch?" *Business Horizons* 37 (July), 55-60.

Farley, John U., and Steven J. Kobrin (1995), "Organizing for the International Marketplace." In *Redesigning the Firm*, eds. Edward H. Bowman and Bruce M. Kogut, 197-216. New York: Oxford University Press.

Farley, John U., and Donald R. Lehmann (1986), *Meta-Analysis in Marketing: Generalization of Response Models*. Lexington, MA: Lexington Books.

Gales, Ron (1995), "Who's on Top?" *Across the Board* (May), 16-21.

George, Michael, Anthony Freeling, and David Court (1994), "Reinventing the Marketing Organization." *The McKinsey Quarterly*, No. 4, 43-62.

Gordon, Robert A., and James E. Howell (1959), *Higher Education for Business*. New York: Columbia University Press.

Greyser, Stephen A. (1972), "Advertising: Attacks and Counters." *Harvard Business Review* 50 (2) (March-April), 22-8, 140-6.

Haeckel, Stephan H. (1995a), "Adaptive Enterprise Design: The Sense and Respond Model." *Planning Review* 23 (May-June).

_____ (1995b), Remarks to a Panel Discussion on Marketing Organizations. Marketing Science Institute Board of Trustees Meeting, Dana Point, California, November 9-10.

_____ and Richard L. Nolan (1993), "Managing by Wire." *Harvard Business Review* 71 (5) (September-October), 122-32.

Hammer, Michael (1996), *Beyond Reengineering: How the Process-Centered Organization Is Changing Our Work and Our Lives.* New York: Harper Business.

Hansen, Ward (1996), "Hits and Misses; Herd Behavior." *Marketing Letters* 7 (October), 297-306.

Harris, T. George (1993), "The Post-Capitalist Executive: An Interview with Peter F. Drucker." *Harvard Business Review* 71 (3) (May-June), 114-22.

Harvard Business Review (1992), "MBA: Is the Traditional Model Doomed?" 70 (6) (November-December), 128-40.

Harvard Business School (1993), "External Comparisons Summary Report: MBA Leadership and Learning." Boston: Harvard Business School Publishing Division Report No. N1-193-149.

Hayes, Robert H., and William J. Abernathy (1980), "Managing Our Way to Economic Decline." *Harvard Business Review* 58 (4) (July-August), 67-77.

Hill, Sam I., David L. Newkirk, and Wayne Henderson (1995), "Dismantling the Brandocracy." *Strategy & Business* (Issue 1) (Fall), 40-53.

Hise, Richard T. (1965), "Have Manufacturing Firms Adopted the Marketing Concept?" *Journal of Marketing* 29 (3) (July), 9-12.

Hunt, Shelby D., and Robert M. Morgan (1995), "The Comparative Advantage Theory of Competition." *Journal of Marketing* 59 (April), 1-15.

Kaldor, Andrew G. (1971), "Imbricative Marketing." *Journal of Marketing* 35 (2) (April), 19-25.

Kallett, Arthur, and F. J. Schlink (1933), *One Hundred Million Guinea Pigs*. New York: Vanguard Press (microform).

Kaminarides, John S., and Roger Roderick (1995), *Journal of Business and Society* 8, 49-61.

Kantor, Erica P., ed. (1995), *Executive MBA Council Membership Directory*.

Karmarkar, Uday S. (1996), "Integrative Research in Marketing and Operations Management." *Journal of Marketing Research* XXXIII (May), 125-33.

Keith, Robert J. (1960), "The Marketing Revolution." *Journal of Marketing* 24 (January), 35-8.

Kiechel, Walter III (1982), "Corporate Strategists under Fire." *Fortune* (December 27), 34-9.

Kohli, Ajay K., and Bernard J. Jaworski (1990), "Market Orientation: The Construct, Research Propositions, and Managerial Implications." *Journal of Marketing* 54 (2) (April), 1-18.

Kordupleski, Raymond E., Roland T. Rust, and Anthony J. Zahorik (1993), "Why Improving Quality Doesn't Improve Quality or Whatever Happened to Marketing." *California Management Review* 35 (3) (Spring), 82-95.

Kotler, Philip (1972), "A Generic Concept of Marketing." *Journal of Marketing* 36 (2) (April), 46-54.

Kotler, Philip, and Sidney J. Levy (1969), "Broadening the Concept of Marketing." *Journal of Marketing* 33 (1) (January), 10-5.

Kwok, Chuck C. Y., Jeffrey Arpan, and William R. Folks, Jr. (1994), "A Global Survey of International Business Education in the 1990s." *Journal of International Business Studies* 25 (3) (Third Quarter), 605-23.

LaLonde, Bernard (1964), "Evolution of the Marketing Concept." In *Toward Scientific Marketing*, ed. Stephen Greyser, 333-43. Chicago: American Marketing Association. Proceedings of Winter Conference of the AMA, Boston, December 27-8, 1963.

Leemon, Daniel O. (1993), "Marketing's Core Role in Strategic Reengineering." *Planning Review* (March/April), 8-13, 46.

Levitt, Theodore (1960), "Marketing Myopia." *Harvard Business Review* (July-August), 45-56.

Levitt, Theodore (1983), "The Globalization of Markets." *Harvard Business Review* 61 (3) (May-June), 92-102.

Liebowitz, S. J., and Stephen E. Margolis (1995), "Path Dependence, Lock-In and History." *Journal of Law, Economics, and Organization* 11 (1) (April), 205-26.

Linder, Jane C., and H. Jeff Smith (1992), "The Complex Case of Management Education." *Harvard Business Review* 70 (5) (September-October), 16-33.

Lodish, Leonard M. (1986), *The Advertising and Promotion Challenge: Vaguely Right or Precisely Wrong?* New York: Oxford University Press.

Lord, Mary (1995), "Getting a Degree by E-Mail." *U.S. News & World Report* (October 30), 91-3.

Low, George S., and Ronald A. Fullerton (1994), "Brands, Brand Management, and the Brand Manager System: A Critical-Historical Evaluation." *Journal of Marketing Research* 31 (2) (May), 173-90.

McCann, John M. (1986), *The Marketing Workbench: Using Computers for Better Performance*. Homewood, IL: Dow Jones-Irwin.

McCarthy, E. Jerome (1960), *Basic Marketing: A Managerial Approach*. Homewood, IL: R.D. Irwin.

McGinn, Daniel (1995), "For Part-Time Students, Golf Will Have to Wait." *New York Times* (September 24), Section 13, 1.

McKenna, Regis (1991), "Marketing Is Everything." *Harvard Business Review* (January-February), 65-79.

McKitterick, John B. (1957), "What Is the Marketing Management Concept?" In *The Frontiers of Marketing Thought and Science*, ed. Frank M. Bass, 71-82. Chicago: American Marketing Association. Proceedings of December 1957 Teachers Conference of the AMA, Philadelphia.

McNamara, Carlton P. (1972), "The Present Status of the Marketing Concept." *Journal of Marketing* 36 (1) (January), 50-7.

Miles, Grant, Charles C. Snow, and Mark P. Sharfman (1993), "Industry Variety and Performance." *Strategic Management Journal* 14 (March), 163-77.

Myers, John G., William F. Massy, and Stephen A. Greyser (1980), *Marketing Research and Knowledge Development: An Assessment for Marketing Management*. Englewood Cliffs, NJ: Prentice Hall.

Nakata, Cheryl, and K. Sivakumar (1995), "Factors in Emerging Markets and Their Impact on First Mover Advantages." Cambridge, MA: Marketing Science Institute, Report No. 95-110.

Nonaka, Ikujiro, and Hirotaka Takeuchi (1995), *The Knowledge-Creating Company*. New York: Oxford University Press.

O'Reilly, Brian (1994), "Reengineering the MBA." *Fortune* (January 24), 38-47.

Packard, Vance (1957), *The Hidden Persuaders*. New York: D. McKay Co.

Parsons, Andrew, Michael Zeisser, and Robert Waitman (1996), "Organizing Today for the Digital Marketing of Tomorrow." McKinsey & Company Presentations to the Harvard Business School Conference on the Future of Interactive Marketing, May 24.

Pierson, Frank C. (1959), *The Education of American Businessmen*. New York: McGraw-Hill.

Pine, B. Joseph (1993), *Mass Customization: The New Frontier in Business Competition*. Boston: Harvard Business School Press.

Prahalad, C. K. (1995), "Weak Signals Versus Strong Paradigms." *Journal of Marketing Research* XXXII (3) (August), iii-viii.

Ruekert, Robert W., Orville C. Walker, Jr., and Kenneth J. Roering (1985), "The Organization of Marketing Activities: A Contingency Theory of Structure and Performance." *Journal of Marketing* 49 (1) (Winter), 13-25.

Russo, J. Edward, and Paul J. H. Schoemaker (1990), *Decision Traps: Ten Barriers to Brilliant Decision-Making and How to Overcome Them*. New York: Simon & Schuster (Fireside).

Schonberger, Richard J. (1992), "Total Quality Management Cuts a Broad Swath—Through Manufacturing and Beyond." *Organizational Dynamics*, 12-21.

Slywotzky, Adrian J. (1996), *Value Migration: How to Think Several Moves Ahead of the Competition*. Boston: Harvard Business School Press. *HG4C28. V3 S57*

Snyder, Thomas D., ed. (1993), *120 Years of American Education: A Statistical Portrait*. Washington, DC: U.S. Department of Education, Office of Educational Research and Improvement, National Center for Education Statistics. (Also World Wide Web at http://www.ed.gov.pubs/stats.html)

Stanton, William J. (1988), "It's Time to Restructure Marketing in Academia." *Journal of Marketing Education* (Summer), 2-7.

Tan, Chin Tiong, and John U. Farley (1987), "The Impact of Cultural Patterns on Cognition and Intention in Singapore." *The Journal of Consumer Research* 13 (4) (March), 540-4.

Treacy, Michael, and Frederick D. Wiersema (1995), *The Discipline of Market Leaders: Choose Your Customers, Narrow Your Focus, Dominate Your Market*. Reading, MA: Addison-Wesley.

Tull, Donald S., Bruce E. Cooley, Mark R. Phillips, Jr., and Harry S. Watkins (1991), "The Organization of Marketing Activities of American Manufacturers." Cambridge, MA: The Marketing Science Institute, Report No. 91-126.

U.S. Bureau of the Census (1994), *Statistical Abstract of the United States: 1994*, 114th ed. Washington, DC: U.S. Bureau of the Census.

Varadarajan, P. Rajan (1992), "Marketing's Contribution to the Strategy Dialogue: The View from a Different Looking Glass." *Journal of the Academy of Marketing Science* 20 (Fall), 335-44.

Virden, Thomas W. (1995), "Can This High-Tech Product Sell Itself?" *Harvard Business Review* 73 (6) (November-December), 24-40.

Watson, Bibi S. (1995), "The New Training Edge." *Management Review* (May), 49-51.

Webster, Frederick E., Jr. (1981), "Top Management's Concerns about Marketing: Issues for the 1980's." *Journal of Marketing* 45 (3) (Summer), 9-16.

_____ (1988), "The Rediscovery of the Marketing Concept." *Business Horizons* 31 (May-June), 29-39.

_____ (1992), "The Changing Role of Marketing in the Corporation." *Journal of Marketing* 56 (4) (October), 1-17.

_____ (1994), *Market-Driven Management: Using the New Marketing Concept to Create a Customer-Oriented Company.* New York: Wiley. HF 5415. 13. W 467

Weitz, Barton, and Erin Anderson (1981), "Organizing the Marketing Function." In *Review of Marketing*, eds. B. Enis and K. Roering, 134-42. Chicago: The American Marketing Association.

Whiteley, Richard C. (1991), *The Customer-Driven Company: Moving From Talk to Action.* Reading, MA: Addison-Wesley.

Workman, John P., Jr. (1993), "Marketing's Limited Role in New Product Development in One Computer Systems Firm." *Journal of Marketing Research* 30 (November), 405-21.

World Bank, *World Tables 1995.* Baltimore, MD: Johns Hopkins University Press.